1000 Ninja Foodi Cookbook for Everyone

Ultimate Ninja Foodi Recipes Cookbook for Beginners & Advanced Users，Quick & Easy Tendercrispy Ninja Foodi Recipes, Live Healthier and Happier

Brandon Jake

Contents

Chapter 3: Healthy Vegetarian And Vegan Recipes 36

Chapter 4: Flavorful Chicken And Poultry Recipes 54

Chapter 5: Savory Beef and Lamb Recipes.............69

Introduction

Welcome to the Complete Guide of Ninja Foodi world! You are going to save your precious time and money regarding cooking your favorite dishes! You are going to have your nutritional and delicious recipes in a short time! You will change your whole life by using a Ninja Foodi, which is really the most multi-functional kitchen appliance in this world now! Everyone should have one! **This book is the perfect companion of your Ninja Foodi cooking!**

Up until the introduction of the Ninja Foodi in 2018, Instant Pots were undoubtedly at the top of the Electric Pressure cooking game while Air Frying was only possible using appliance that was specifically designed for Air Frying, such as the ones from Philips.

Even though the Instant Pot could replace most of the everyday kitchen appliances such as Saute Pan, Steamer, Slow Cooker, etc., the one thing that it wasn't able to do, was replicate the effects of an Air Fryer.

And this is exactly where the revolutionary Ninja Foodi came in and completely flipped the paradigm with its revolutionary new "**TenderCrisp**" technology! At its heart, the amazing Ninja Foodi is an all-in-one kitchen appliance like that no other, that is designed to replace not only an Instant Pot and CrockPot but also an Air Fryer! The meticulously crafted design of this single appliance allows you to Saute, Broil, Bake, Roast, Pressure Cook, Steam, Slow Cook and even Air Fry! All under the same hood.

This Ninja Foodi can accomplish this feat, thanks to the crisping lid that comes attached with the Foodi itself. When needed, this particular lid alongside the Air Crisp Function and Crisping Basket allows the users to seamless Air Fry their dishes and give them a satisfying crispy finish!

Throughout the first chapter of the book, you will find that I have discussed the core concepts of the Ninja Foodi in greater details, so if this is your first time diving into the world of Ninja Foodi, **this is the perfect opportunity to get the hang of this amazing device!**

And once you are done with the introduction and chaprer 1, feel free to explore the amazing Ninja Foodi recipes found in this booklet and let your creativity go wild!

Welcome, to the world of amazing Ninja Foodi cooking!

Chapter 1: All Essentials of Ninja Foodi

What's the Ninja Foodi

The Ninja Foodie is probably the most versatile, and undoubtedly revolutionary kitchen appliance out there in the market.

This is the only appliance of its kind that can work as Slow Cooker, Saute pan, Electric Pressure Cooker, Rice Cooker, and even an Air Fryer! All under one hood.

The unique technology that allows its designers to blend the functionalities of Air Fryer and Pressure Cooker means that chefs can cook their food more efficiently and faster than any other kitchen appliance to date.

And just in case you are wondering, with this amazing device, you won't only be limited to simple pressure cooker dishes! The versatility of this appliance will allow you to create anything from soups, stews, chili's to breakfast and desserts! Your imagination is the only limitation here.

For new beginners though, the barrage of functionalities might seem a little bit confusing at first, but rest assured, the appliance is very easy to use.

All you need is a little understanding of what each function button does, and you are good to go!

Ninja Foodi VS. Instant Pot/Slow Cooker/Air Fryer

At its heart, the core difference between all three of the above-mentioned appliances and the Ninja Foodi is that the Ninja Foodi is the combination of all three. Meaning, with this revolutionary appliance, you will be able to Pressure Cook, Slow Cook, and even Air Fryer your meals with ease.

Asides from that, there are some fundamental differences that you should about as well.

Considering the Ninja Foodi and Air Fryer: The Air Fryer is essentially an appliance that is strictly designed for just the purpose of Air Frying various and preparing various meals, using the minimum amount of oil. This appliance is excellent at what it does and using an Air Fryer; you can prepare a plethora of different types of meals. However, it is not an all in one.

Comparing the Ninja Foodi with an Air Fryer, you would immediately notice that they both sport a very distinctive shape. The Ninja Foodi is like a round pot, similar to the Instant Pot while the Air Fryer extrudes a little a bit on the top side.

The Crisping Lid alongside the TenderCrisp technology that allows the Ninja Foodi to Air Fry meals, while working as an advanced and versatile is what sets it apart from the Air Fryer.

Considering the Ninja Foodi and Instant Pot and Slow Cooker: The Slow Cooker and Instant Pot are probably the two appliances can be considered as being the closest sibling to the Ninja Foodi Electric Pressure cooker!

All three of the appliances sport a similar shape, which is like a pot.

However, general Slow Cookers are only designed to do just one thing, that is to cook your meals for an extended period at extremely low temperatures. (There are multifunctional Slow Cookers, but we are not considering them here).

Instant Pots, on the other hand, are multifunctional Electric Pressure Cookers, which were pretty much the king of the game until the arrival of the Ninja Foodi, which might dethrone them. Similar to the Ninja Foodi, Instant Pot's also come packed with a large number of different features that allows users to bake, roast, simmer, boil, steam and pressure cook their meals.

However, the crucial point where the Ninja Foodi stands out is that alongside most of the features of the Instant Pot and Slow Cooker, the Ninja Foodi is capable of Air Frying meals using the Crisping Lid and TenderCrisp technology.

So in short, the Ninja Foodi is essentially the combination of all three appliances in on nifty package.

Uncover Secret of the Revolutionary Tendercrisp Technology

The Tendercrisp Technology stands at the heart of the Ninja Foodi cooking appliance that seemingly differentiates itself from the rest of the world. So, I strongly believe that it is really important that you have a good understanding of what this unique technology does.

So when you are pressure cooking tough ingredients such as meats, you end up with meals that are extremely juicy and satisfying to eat, but tender as well. Just pressure cooking alone won't be able to provide you with any crispy finish! This is where Air Frying comes in.

Air Frying utilizes the power of air to make foods crispier by giving it a nice tasty crust.

The revolutionary technology used in the Ninja Foodi allows a user to infuse both the effects of Pressure Cooking and Air Frying using just the single device! This basic cooking principle of combining both cooking methods is known as Ninja Foodi's proprietary TenderCrisp Technology.

In short, it allows you to create meals that are extremely tender and juicy on the side while having a satisfying crust on the surface.

The basic cooking procedure will ask you first to cook you a meal using pressure cooking, then use the Crisping Lid and Crisping Basket accompanied by the Air Crisp function to achieve your desired level of crispiness.

To better understand the mechanism at work here, the TenderCrisp technology utilizes superheated steam to infuse both flavors and moisture into your pressure cooked food.

Afterward, the crisping lid blows extremely hot air to every side of your meal that gives it a fine golden color and crisp finish.

This unique combination is so far unachievable by any other appliance to date!

Different Function Buttons of the Ninja Foodi

Given the versatility of the Ninja Foodi, it is very easy to understand why some individuals might get confused when dealing with the plethora of amazing functions available in the appliance.

To make things easier for you and ensure that you don't have to face any troubles in the future, I have tried to outline the basic functions of all of the buttons present in most models of the Ninja Foodi.

Pressure

Let's first talk about the single feature that you will be using most of the time. The Pressure function will allow you to use your Ninja Foodi as a Pressure Cooker appliance and cook your meals as you would in an electric pressure cooker such as the Instant Pot.

In this feature, foods are cooked at high temperature under pressure.

Just make sure to be careful when releasing the pressure! Otherwise, you might harm yourself. There are essentially two ways through which you can release the pressure, which is discussed later on in the chapter.

Steam

Asides from Air Crisp, the Steam Function is probably one of the healthiest cooking option available in the Foodi!

The basic principle is as follows- Water is boiled inside the Ninja Foodi that generates a good amount of steam. This hot steam is then used to cook your ingredients kept in a steaming rack situated at the top of the inner chamber of your Pot.

Steaming is perfect for vegetables and other tender foods as it allows to preserve the nutrients while maintaining a nice crispy perfectly.

Asides from vegetables, however, the Steam function can also be used for cooking various fish and seafood, which are much more delicate than other red meats and chicken.

The process of steaming fish are the same, all you have to do is place them on the steaming rack. Steaming the fish helps to preserve the flavor and moisture as well perfectly.

Slow Cooker

Despite popular belief, some foods tend to taste a whole lot better when Slowly Cooked over extremely low temperature for hours on end. This is why Slow Cookers such as the CrockPot are so popular amongst chefs and house makers!

The Slow Cooker feature of the Ninja Foodi allows you to achieve the same result, but without the need for a different appliance.

Ideal scenarios to use the Slow Cooker function would be when you want to cook your foods for longer to bring out the intense flavor of spices and herbs in stews, soups, and casseroles.

Since it takes a lot of time to Slow Cook, you should prepare and toss the ingredients early on before your feeding time.

For example. If you want to have your Slow Cooker meal for breakfast, prepare ingredients the night before and add them to your Foodi. The Foodi will do its magic and have the meal prepared by morning.

The Slow Cooker feature also comes with a HIGH or LOW setting that allows you to decide how long you want your meal to simmer.

Start/Stop Button

The function of this particular button is pretty straightforward; it allows you to initiate or stop the cooking process.

Sear/Saute

The Browning/Saute or Sear/Saute mode of the Ninja Foodi provides you with the means to brown your meat before cooking it using a just a little bit of oil. This is similar to when you are browning meat on a stovetop frying pan. And keeping that in mind, the Ninja Foodie's browning mode comes with five different Stove Top temperature settings that allow you to set your desired settings with ease.

Asides from browning meat, the different Stove Top temperatures also allows you to gently simmer your foods, cook or even sear them at very high temperatures.

Searing is yet another way to infuse the delicious flavors of your meat inside and give an extremely satisfying result.

This particular model is also excellent if you are in the mode for a quick Sautéed vegetable snack to go along with your main course.

Air Crisp

This is probably the feature that makes the Ninja Foodi so revolutionary and awesome to use! The Tendercrisp lid that comes as a part of the Ninja Foodi allows you to use the appliance as the perfect Air Fryer device.

Using the Tendercrisp lid and Air Crisp mode, the appliance will let you bake, roast, broil meals to perfection using just the power of superheated air! In the end, you will get perfectly caramelized, heartwarming dishes.

The Foodi comes with a dedicated crisping basket that is specifically designed for this purpose, which optimizes the way meals are air fried in the Foodi.

But the best part in all of these is probably the fact that the using the Air Crisp feature, you will be able to cook your meals using almost none to minimal amount of oil!

It is also possible to combine both the pressure cooking mechanism and Air Crisp function to create unique and flavorful dishes.

The Pressure cooking phase will help you to seal the delicious juices of the meal inside the meat, while the crisping lid and Air Crisp mechanism will provide you to cook/roast your meal to perfection, giving a nice heartfelt crispy finish.

This combined method is also amazing when roasting whole chicken meat or roasts, as all the moisture remains intact and the final result turns out to be a dramatic crispy finish.

Bake/Roast

For anyone who loves to bake, this function is a dream come true! The Bake/Roast function allows the Foodi to be used as a traditional convection oven. This means you will be do anything that you might do with a general everyday oven! If you are in the mode to bake amazing cakes or casseroles, the Foodi has got you covered!

Broil

The main purpose of the Broil function is to allow you to use your appliance like an oven broiler and slightly brown the top of your dish if required. If you are in the mood for roasting a fine piece of pork loin to perfection or broiling your dish until the cheese melts and oozes, this mode is the perfect one to go with!

Dehydrate

In some more premium models of the Ninja Foodi appliance, you will notice a function labeled as "Dehydrate." This particular function is best suited for simple dried snacks such as dried apple slices, banana chips, jerky, etc. As you can probably guess, the core idea of this function is to suck out the moisture and dehydrate your ingredient into a hearty edible snack.

The Different Parts and Accessories of the Ninja Foodi

THE NINJA FOODI

Pressure Release Valve
Easily release pressure.

Pressure Lid
Quickly tenderize and cook ingredients.

Reversible Rack
Use to steam, or reverse to broil.

Cook & Crisp Basket
4-quart nonstick, ceramic-coated basket fits 3 lbs of French fries.

Crisping Lid
Use to finish off pressure cooked recipes or to air fry your food.

Cooking Pot
6.5-quart nonstick, ceramic-coated cooking pot, fits a 6-lb roast.

14 Levels of Safety
Passed rigorous testing to earn UL safety certification, giving you peace of mind.

The different parts of the Ninja Foodi are as follows:

- **Pressure Release Valve:** These valves are used to control the entrapment or release of the pressure inside the pot.
- **Pressure Lid:** The pressure lid is used when pressure is cooking your meals.
- **Crisping Lid:** The crisping lid is used when trying to Air Fryer your meals using the TenderCrisp technology.
- **Cooking Pot:** The cooking pot is the actual inner pot where you dump the ingredients and let it cook.

Asides from the above-mentioned core parts, there are some others that you should know about as well.

The Reversible Rack: This particular rack can be used both ways for your desired effect. The reversible rack is primarily used for broiling (when placed in the upper position), while it can also be used for steaming, cooking, baking, and roasting, should you choose to place it in the lower position.

Cook And Crisp Basket: The crisping basket is an easily removable basket that is specially designed for Air Crisping.

Various other accessories are also available for the Ninja Foodi. Some of the more useful ones are as follows:

Extra Reversible Rack/ 8 Inch Round Wire Cooling Rack: Some recipes might ask you to use a rack twice, once for steaming and once for broiling for example. Instead of using the same rack over and over again, it's a pretty good idea to have an extra rack around, and it makes life a whole lot easier.

And as a bonus, you will also be able to use it as a cooling rack as well.

Extra Sealing Ring: Overtime and despite your best efforts, the Silicone ring might pick up dirt and unpleasant odor. Despite its pretty long-lasting durability, they tend to become nicked or stretched after prolonged usage!

Having a damaged or compromised Sealing Ring is never a good idea as it will render your pot useless in the future. Therefore, keeping an extra ring always helps in the long run. You When buying an extra ring, make sure to check that you are buying a ring that is specifically designed for the Foodi. Otherwise, it won't fit properly.

Multi-Purpose Pan/Metal/Ceramic Bowl: If you do a lot of Pot-In-Pot cooking, then having a ceramic or metal bowl would be a Godsend! These are excellent for when you are making dishes such as quiches, casseroles or even cake. Just make sure to buy a one that it no more than about 8 and ½ inches across. The official Multi-Purpose Pan sold by Ninja is excellent for this purpose.

Roasting Rack Insert: This rack is specifically designed to work with the Cook and Crisp Basket, and comes in real handy if you want to roast or glaze meat/ribs.

Cook and Crisp Layered Insert: This layout helps to increase the capacity of the Cook and Crisp Basket by allowing you to create layers of meals and crisp them all at once.

Amazing advantages of the Ninja Foodi

At its heart, the Ninja Foodi is an electric pressure cooker, and making foods utilizing this single aspect will yield you extremely juicy and tender meals in no time!

But why should you limit yourself to only that?

Asides from being able to prepare mouthwatering pressure cooked and fried air meals, the Ninja Foodi comes with a plethora of advantages that will make your cooking experience even more delightful.

Below are just some of the many!

Allows you to cook frozen food: With the awesome power of the Ninja Foodi, you will be able to save a huge amount of time by skipping the "defrosting" phase and adding your meat right out of the freezer! The advanced cooking technologies allow the Foodi to defrost the meat and cook them to perfection in no time!

Let's you cook healthier meals: The precise cooking mechanism of the Ninja Foodi allows the appliance to preserve most of the nutrition of your meal while ensuring that your meals are undeniably delicious.

Acts as a one-stop shop: This single appliance acts as a one-stop shop for all of your meals! You can cook, roast, steam in the single pot itself and have everything ready by the end!

Allows cooking in a single pot: Just using a single pot, you will be able to convert a simple and regular looking soup into an amazing casserole dish or something exquisite. The versatility of the Ninja Foodi means that you won't have to use multiple pots for your cooking, the single pot provided with the Foodi is more than enough to prepare your meal from scratch to finish.

Frees up a lot of kitchen space: Regardless o the size of your kitchen, the ergonomic design of the Ninja Foodi means that you will always be able to make up space for this nifty appliance! And since this pot can perform the job of a Slow Cooker, Air Fryer, Pressure Cooker, etc. all alone, you won't even have to keep any other appliances around!

Easy Cleaning: Cleaning is a nightmare for every chef and homemaker! Since all the cooking is done in a ceramic coated non-stick pot in the Ninja Foodi, cleaning the appliance is a breeze! All it takes is a little bit of soapy water, and you are good to go!

Kills Any And All Harmful Micro-Organism: Sophisticated Electric Pressure Cookers such as the Ninja Foodi allows the internal temperature inside the pot to reach extremely high levels! This allows the pot to destroy most viruses and bacteria that might otherwise be harmful to your body. Some of the more resistant ones found in raw maize or corns can also be destroyed as well.

Useful Tips for Ninja Foodi Cooking

As time goes on, you will learn how to utilize the power of your Ninja Foodi to its full extent. However, the following tips will help you during the early days of your life with the Foodi and ensure that your experience is as pleasant and smooth as possible.

- It is crucial that you don't just press the function buttons randomly! Try to read through the function of each button and use them according to the requirement of your recipe.
- This is something that many people don't know, once the cooking timer of your appliance hits '0', the pot will automatically go into "Natural Pressure Release" mode where it will start to release the pressure on its own. You can use a quick release anytime to release all the steam at once, or you can wait for 10-15 minutes until the steam vents off.
- It is important that you place the lid properly while closing the appliance as it greatly affects the cooking. Therefore, make sure that your lid is tightly close by ensuring that the silicone ring inside the lid is placed all the way around the groove.
- If you are in a rush and want to release the pressure quickly, turn the pressure valve to "Open Position," which will quick release all the pressure. But this can be a little risky as a lot of steam comes out at once, so be sure to stay careful.
- Once your start using the appliance for cooking, make sure to check if the Pressure Valve is in the "Locked Position." If it is not, your appliance won't be able to build up pressure inside for cooking.
- If you are dealing with a recipe that calls for unfrozen meat, make sure to use the same amount of cooking time and liquid that you would use if you were to use frozen meat of the same type.
- Make sure to keep in mind that the "Timer" button isn't a button to set time! Rather it acts as a Delay Timer. Using this button, you will be able to set a specific time, after which the Ninja Foodi will automatically wake up and start cooking the food.

Frequently Asked Questions

Below are the answers to some of the most commonly asked questions that should help you clear up some confusion (if you have any).

Why do some foods such as rice, or veggies call for different cooking times in different recipes?

The cooking time does not only depend on the type of ingredient that you are using but on various other factors as well.
When considering vegetables, you have to consider how the veggies are cut. If using a whole cauliflower head, it might be cubed, cut into florets, alternatively, you can have cubed potatoes and whole potatoes.
Cubed variations will always take less time than the whole veggie itself.
The same goes for meat as well, the thickness and the cut largely vary the time taken to cooking the meal properly.

If you are cooking rice, you might be interested to know that pressure cooking rice directly into the pot will cook much faster than pressure cooking the rice in a bowl that is set on the rack.

Is it possible to adjust the temperature of Sautéing or Searing?

Yes, all you have to do is press the Temperature Up and Down arrows twice, and the appliance will change the heat setting and allow you to Saute/Sear at your selected mode.

Is Pre-heating necessary when using the Crisping or Roasting feature?

It is not necessary that you preheat your pot, if you do, you will get better results. Just let the appliance pre-heat for 5 minutes before cooking.

Is it possible to open the lid while cooking?

As long as you are using any of the convection methods such as Air Crisp, Bake/Roast, you are allowed to open the lid at any time you want. Once you open up the lid, the cooking will pause and will only resume once you have securely placed the lid.
However, while Pressure Cooking/Steaming, you should never open the lid until the whole cook cycle and pressure release cycle is complete!

Are the different parts of the Foodi Dishwasher safe?

Yes, all the accessories of the Ninja Foodi are dishwasher safe, alongside the inner pot as well. However, keep in mind that the base, Crisping Lid, and Pressure Lid are NOT dishwasher safe and should be cleaned by using a sponge or wet cloth.

How to get rid of the unpleasant smell from the Sealing Ring?

The most basic step to do is to remove the sealing ring after every cook session and washing/drying I before putting it back. You can do this either by hand or by using your dishwasher. If that doesn't do the trick, try to leave it under the sun for a while.

Chapter 2: Delicious Breakfast Recipes

The Early Morning Veggie Hash Brown
(Prepping time: 10 minutes\ Cooking time: 20 minutes |For 3 servings)

Ingredients

- 1 tablespoon unsalted butter
- ½ teaspoon dried thyme, crushed
- ½ cup cauliflower florets, boiled and chopped
- ½ small on ion, chopped
- ½ cup water
- Salt and pepper to taste
- ½ pound turkey meat, chopped
- ¼ cup heavy cream

Directions

1. Set your Ninja Foodi to Saute mode and let it heat up, add butter and let the butter melt
2. Add onion and Saute for 3 minutes
3. Add chopped cauliflowers
4. Saute for 2 minutes longer
5. Add turkey and water
6. Close Pressure lid and set your Ninja Foodi to HIGH pressure mode, cook for 10 minutes
7. Quick release the pressure
8. Set the Ninja Foodie to BROIL mode (lid open) and add heavy cream, close the lid and let it Broil for 2 minutes
9. Serve and enjoy!

Nutrition Values (Per Serving)

- Calories: 151
- Fat: 11g
- Carbohydrates: 0.7g
- Protein: 11g

Sicilian Cauliflower Roast Crunch
(Prepping time: 10 minutes\ Cooking time: 10 minutes |For 4 servings)

Ingredients

- 1 medium cauliflower head, leaves removed
- ¼ cup olive oil
- 1 teaspoon red pepper, crushed
- ½ cup water
- 2 tablespoons capers, rinsed and minced
- ½ cup parmesan cheese, grated
- 1 tablespoon fresh parsley, chopped

Directions

1. Prepare the Ninja Foodi by adding water and place the cook and crisp basket inside the pot
2. Cut an "X" on the head of cauliflower by using a knife and slice it about halfway down
3. Take a basket and transfer the cauliflower in it
4. Then put on the pressure lid and seal it and set it on low pressure for 3 minutes
5. Add olive oil, capers, garlic, and crushed red pepper into it and mix them well
6. Once the cauliflower is cooked, do a quick release and remove the lid
7. Pour in the oil and spice mixture on the cauliflower
8. Spread equally on the surface then sprinkle some Parmesan cheese from the top
9. Close the pot with crisping lid
10. Set it on Air Crisp mode to 390 degrees F for 10 minutes
11. Once done, remove the cauliflower flower the Ninja Foodi transfer it into a serving plate
12. Cut it up into pieces and transfer them to serving plates
13. Sprinkle fresh parsley from the top
14. Serve and enjoy!

Nutrition Values (Per Serving)

- Calories: 119
- Fat: 10g
- Carbohydrates: 5g
- Protein: 2.2g

Heartfelt Spinach Quiche

(Prepping time: 10 minutes\ Cooking time: 33 minutes |For 4 servings)

Ingredients

- 1 tablespoon butter, melted
- 1 pack (10 ounces) frozen spinach, thawed
- 5 organic eggs, beaten
- Salt and pepper to taste

- 3 cups Monterey Jack Cheese, shredded

Directions

1. Set your Ninja Foodi to Saute mode and let it heat up, add butter and let the butter melt
2. Add spinach and Saute for 3 minutes, transfer the Sautéed spinach to a bowl
3. Add eggs, cheese, salt and pepper to a bowl and mix it well
4. Transfer the mixture to greased quiche molds and transfer the mold to your Foodi
5. Close lid and choose the "Bake/Roast" mode and let it cook for 30 minutes at 360 degrees F
6. Once done, open lid and transfer the dish out
7. Cut into wedges and serve
8. Enjoy!

Nutrition Values (Per Serving)

- Calories: 349
- Fat: 27g
- Carbohydrates: 3.2g
- Protein: 23g

Breakfast Broccoli Casserole
(Prepping time: 10 minutes\ Cooking time: 7 minutes |For 4 servings)

Ingredients

- 1 tablespoon extra-virgin olive oil
- 1 pound broccoli, cut into florets
- 1 pound cauliflower, cut into florets
- ¼ cup almond flour
- 2 cups coconut milk
- ½ teaspoon ground nutmeg
- Pinch of pepper
- 1 and ½ cup shredded Gouda cheese, divided

Directions

1. Pre-heat your Ninja Foodi by setting it to Saute mode
2. Add olive oil and let it heat up, add broccoli and cauliflower
3. Take a medium bowl stir in almond flour, coconut milk, nutmeg, pepper, 1 cup cheese and add the mixture to your Ninja Foodi
4. Top with ½ cup cheese and lock lid, cook on HIGH pressure for 5 minutes
5. Release pressure naturally over 10 minutes

6. Serve and enjoy!

Nutrition Values (Per Serving)

- Calories: 373
- Fat: 32g
- Carbohydrates: 6g
- Protein: 16g

Tantalizing Beef Jerky
(Prepping time: 10 minutes\ Cooking time: 20 minutes |For 4 servings)

Ingredients

- ½ pound beef, sliced into 1/8 inch thick strips
- ½ cup of soy sauce
- 2 tablespoons Worcestershire sauce
- 2 teaspoons ground black pepper
- 1 teaspoon onion powder
- ½ teaspoon garlic powder
- 1 teaspoon salt

Directions

1. Add listed ingredient to a large-sized Ziploc bag, seal it shut
2. Shake well, leave it in the fridge overnight
3. Lay strips on dehydrator trays, making sure not to overlap them
4. Lock Air Crisping Lid and set the temperature to 135 degrees F, cook for 7 hours
5. Store in airtight container, enjoy!

Nutrition Values (Per Serving)

- Calories: 62
- Fat: 7g
- Carbohydrates: 2g
- Protein: 9g

Beefed Up Spaghetti Squash
(Prepping time: 5 minutes\ Cooking time: 10-15 minutes |For 4 servings)

Ingredients

- 2 pounds ground beef
- 1 medium spaghetti squash

- 32 ounces marinara sauce
- 3 tablespoons olive oil

Directions

1. Slice squash in half lengthwise and dispose of seeds
2. Add trivet to your Ninja Foodi
3. Add 1 cup water
4. Arrange squash on the rack and lock lid, cook on HIGH pressure for 8 minutes
5. Quick release pressure
6. Remove from pot
7. Clean pot and set your Ninja Foodi to Saute mode
8. Add ground beef and add olive oil, let it heat up
9. Add ground beef and cook until slightly browned and cooked
10. Separate strands from cooked squash and transfer to a bowl
11. Add cooked beef, and mix with marinara sauce
12. Serve and enjoy!

Nutrition Values (Per Serving)

- Calories: 174
- Fat: 6g
- Carbohydrates: 5g
- Protein: 19g

Adobo Cubed Steak

(Prepping time: 5 minutes\ Cooking time: 25 minutes |For 4 servings)

Ingredients

- 2 cups of water
- 8 steaks, cubed, 28 ounces pack
- Pepper to taste
- 1 and ¾ teaspoons adobo seasoning
- 1 can (8 ounces) tomato sauce
- 1/3 cup green pitted olives
- 2 tablespoons brine
- 1 small red pepper
- ½ a medium onion, sliced

Directions

1. Chop peppers, onions into ¼ inch strips
2. Prepare beef by seasoning with adobo and pepper
3. Add into Ninja Foodi
4. Add remaining ingredients and Lock lid, cook on HIGH pressure for 25 minutes
5. Release pressure naturally
6. Serve and enjoy!

Nutrition Values (Per Serving)

- Calories: 154
- Fat: 5g
- Carbohydrates: 3g
- Protein: 23g

Cool Beef Bourguignon

(Prepping time: 10 minutes\ Cooking time: 30 minutes |For 4 servings)

Ingredients

- 1 pound stewing steak
- ½ pound bacon
- 5 medium carrots, diced
- 1 large red onion, peeled and sliced
- 2 garlic cloves, minced
- 2 teaspoons salt
- 2 tablespoons fresh thyme
- 2 tablespoons fresh parsley
- 2 teaspoons ground pepper
- ½ cup beef broth
- 1 tablespoon olive oil
- 1 tablespoon sugar-free maple syrup (Keto friendly)

Directions

1. Set your Ninja Foodi to Saute mode and add 1 tablespoon of oil, allow the oil to heat up
2. Pat your beef dry and season it well
3. Add beef into the Ninja Foodi (in batches) and Saute them until nicely browned up
4. Slice up the cooked bacon into strips and add the strips to the pot
5. Add onions as well and brown them
6. Add the rest of the listed ingredients and lock up the lid
7. Cook for 30 minutes on HIGH pressure

8. Allow the pressure to release naturally over 10 minutes

9. Enjoy!

Nutrition Values (Per Serving)

- Calories: 416
- Fats: 18g
- Carbs: 12g
- Protein:27g

A Keto-Friendly Philly Willy Steak And Cheese

(Prepping time: 10 minutes\ Cooking time: 40 minutes |For 4 servings)

Ingredients

- 2 tablespoons olive oil
- 2 large onion, sliced
- 8 ounces mushrooms, sliced
- 1-2 teaspoons Keto friendly steak seasoning
- 1 tablespoon butter
- 2 pounds beef chuck roast
- 12 cup beef stock

Directions

1. Set your Ninja Foodi to Saute mode and add oil, let it heat up

2. Rub seasoning over roast and Saute for 1-2 minutes per side

3. Remove and add butter, onion

4. Add mushrooms, pepper, stock, and roast

5. Lock lid and cook on HIGH pressure for 35 minutes

6. Naturally, release pressure over 10 minutes

7. Shred meat and sprinkle cheese if using, enjoy!

Nutrition Values (Per Serving)

- Calories: 425
- Fats: 25g
- Carbs: 3g
- Protein: 46g

Beef Stew

(Prepping time: 10 minutes\ Cooking time: 10 minutes |For 4 servings)

Ingredients

- 1 pound beef roast
- 4 cups beef broth
- 3 garlic cloves, chopped
- 1 carrot, chopped
- 2 celery stalks, chopped
- 2 tomatoes, chopped
- ½ white onion, chopped
- ¼ teaspoon salt
- 1/8 teaspoon ground black pepper

Directions

1. Add listed ingredients to your Ninja Foodi and lock lid, cook on HIGH pressure for 10 minutes
2. Quick release pressure
3. Open the lid and shred the bee using forks, serve and enjoy!

Nutrition Values (Per Serving)

- Calories: 211
- Fat: 7g
- Carbohydrates: 2g
- Protein: 10g

Juiciest Keto Bacon Strips

(Prepping time: 5 minutes\ Cooking time: 7 minutes |For 2 servings)

Ingredients

- 10 bacon strips
- ¼ teaspoon chili flakes
- 1/3 teaspoon salt
- ¼ teaspoon basil, dried

Directions

1. Rub the bacon strips with chili flakes, dried basil, and salt

2. Turn on your air fryer and place the bacon on the rack

3. Lower the air fryer lid

4. Cook the bacon at 400F for 5 minutes

5. Cook for 3 minutes more if the bacon is not fully cooked

6. Serve and enjoy!

Nutrition Values (Per Serving)

- Calories: 500
- Fat: 46g
- Carbohydrates: 0g
- Protein: 21g

Quick Picadillo Dish

(Prepping time: 10 minutes\ Cooking time: 15-20 minutes |For 4 servings)

Ingredients

- ½ pound lean ground beef
- 2 garlic cloves, minced
- ½ large onion, chopped
- 1 teaspoon salt
- 1 tomato, chopped
- ½ red bell pepper, chopped
- 1 tablespoon cilantro
- ½ can (4 ounces) tomato sauce
- 1 teaspoon ground cumin
- 1-2 bay leaves
- 2 tablespoons green olives, capers
- 2 tablespoons brine
- 3 tablespoons water

Directions

1. Set your Ninja Foodi to Saute mode and add meat, salt, and pepper, slightly brown

2. Add garlic, tomato, onion, cilantro and Saute for 1 minute

3. Add olives, brine, leaf, cumin, and mix

4. Pour in sauce, water, and stir

5. Lock lid and cook on HIGH pressure for 15 minutes

6. Quick release pressure

Nutrition Values (Per Serving)

- Calories: 207
- Fats: 8g
- Carbs: 4g
- Protein: 25g

Simple/Aromatic Meatballs

(Prepping time: 8 minutes\ Cooking time: 11 minutes |For 4 servings)

Ingredients

- 2 cups ground beef
- 1 egg, beaten
- 1 teaspoon Taco seasoning
- 1 tablespoon sugar-free marinara sauce
- 1 teaspoon garlic, minced
- ½ teaspoon salt

Directions

1. Take a big mixing bowl and place all the ingredients into the bowl
2. Add all the ingredients into the bowl
3. Mix together all the ingredients by using a spoon or fingertips
4. Then make the small size meatballs and put them in a layer in the air fryer rack
5. Lower the air fryer lid
6. Cook the meatballs for 11 minutes at 350 F
7. Serve immediately and enjoy!

Nutrition Values (Per Serving)

- Calories: 205
- Fat: 12.2g
- Carbohydrates: 2.2g
- Protein: 19.4g

Generous Shepherd's Pie

(Prepping time: 10 minutes\ Cooking time: 10-15 minutes |For 4 servings)

Ingredients

- 2 cups of water

- 4 tablespoons butter
- 4 ounces cream cheese
- 1 cup mozzarella
- 1 whole egg
- Salt and pepper to taste
- 1 tablespoon garlic powder
- 2-3 pounds ground beef
- 1 cup frozen carrots
- 8 ounces mushrooms, sliced
- 1 cup beef broth

Directions

1. Add water to Ninja Foodi, arrange cauliflower on top, lock lid and cook for 5 minutes on HIGH pressure

2. Quick release and transfer to a blender, add cream cheese, butter, mozzarella cheese, egg, pepper, and salt. Blend well

3. Drain water from Ninja Foodi and add beef

4. Add carrots, garlic powder, broth and pepper, and salt

5. Add in cauliflower mix and lock lid, cook for 10 minutes on HIGH pressure

6. Release pressure naturally over 10 minutes

7. Serve and enjoy!

Nutrition Values (Per Serving)

- Calories: 303
- Fats: 21g
- Carbs: 4g
- Protein: 21g

Creamy Early Morning Asparagus Soup

(Prepping time: 10 minutes\ Cooking time: 5-10 minutes |For 4 servings)

Ingredients

- 1 tablespoon olive oil
- 3 green onions, sliced crosswise into ¼ inch pieces
- 1 pound asparagus, tough ends removed, cut into 1 inch pieces
- 4 cups vegetable stock
- 1 tablespoon unsalted butter
- 1 tablespoon almond flour

- 2 teaspoon salt
- 1 teaspoon white pepper
- ½ cup heavy cream

Directions

1. Set your Ninja Foodi to "Saute" mode and add oil, let it heat up
2. Add green onions and Saute for a few minutes, add asparagus and stock
3. Lock lid and cook on HIGH pressure for 5 minutes
4. Take a small saucepan and place it over low heat, add butter, flour and stir until the mixture foams and turns into a golden beige, this is your blond roux
5. Remove from heat
6. Release pressure naturally over 10 minutes
7. Open lid and add roux, salt and pepper to the soup
8. Use an immersion blender to puree the soup
9. Taste and season accordingly, swirl in cream and enjoy!

Nutrition Values (Per Serving)
- Calories: 192
- Fat: 14g
- Carbohydrates: 8g
- Protein: 6g

Good-Day Pumpkin Puree

(Prepping time: 10 minutes\ Cooking time: 13-15 minutes |For 2 servings)

Ingredients

- 2 pounds small sized pumpkin, halved and seeded
- ½ cup water
- Salt and pepper to taste

Directions

1. Add water to your Ninja Foodi, place steamer rack in the pot
2. Add pumpkin halves to the rack and lock lid, cook on HIGH pressure for 13-15 minutes
3. Once done, quick release pressure and let the pumpkin cool
4. Once done, scoop out flesh into a bowl
5. Blend using an immersion blender and season with salt and pepper
6. Serve and enjoy!

Nutrition Values (Per Serving)
- Calories: 112
- Fat: 2g

- Carbohydrates: 7g
- Protein: 2g

Amazing Bacon And Veggie Delight

(Prepping time: 5 minutes\ Cooking time: 25 minutes |For 4 servings)

Ingredients

- 1 green bell pepper, chopped
- 4 bacon slices
- ½ cup parmesan cheese
- 1 tablespoon avocado mayonnaise (Keto Friendly)
- 2 scallions, chopped

Directions

1. Arrange your bacon slices in your Ninja Foodi pot and top them up with avocado mayo, scallions, bell peppers, parmesan cheese
2. Close lid and select the Bake/Roast mode, set timer to 25 minutes and temperature to 365 degrees F
3. Let it bake and remove the dish after 25 minutes
4. Serve and enjoy!

Nutrition Values (Per Serving)

- Calories: 197
- Fat: 13g
- Carbohydrates: 5g
- Protein: 14g

Hearty Broccoli And Scrambled Cheese Breakfast

(Prepping time: 10 minutes\ Cooking time: 5 minutes |For 4 servings)

Ingredients

- 1 pack, 12 ounces frozen broccoli florets
- 2 tablespoons butter
- salt and pepper as needed
- 8 whole eggs

- 2 tablespoons milk
- ¾ cup white cheddar cheese, shredded
- Crushed red pepper, as needed

Directions

1. Add butter and broccoli to your Ninja Foodi
2. Season with salt and pepper according to your taste
3. Set the Ninja to Medium Pressure mode and let it cook for about 10 minutes, covered, making sure to keep stirring the broccoli from time to time
4. Take a medium sized bowl and add crack in the eggs, beat the eggs gently
5. Pour milk into the eggs and give it a nice stir
6. Add the egg mixture into the Ninja (over broccoli) and gently stir, cook for 2 minutes (uncovered)
7. Once the egg has settled in, add cheese and sprinkle red pepper, black pepper, and salt
8. Enjoy with bacon strips if you prefer!

Nutrition Values (Per Serving)

- Calories: 184
- Fat: 12g
- Carbohydrates: 5g
- Protein: 12g

Original Onion And Scrambled Tofu
(Prepping time: 8 minutes\ Cooking time: 12 minutes |For 4 servings)

Ingredients

- 4 tablespoons butter
- 2 tofu blocks, pressed and cubed in to 1 inch pieces
- Salt and pepper to taste
- 1 cup cheddar cheese, grated
- 2 medium onions, sliced

Directions

1. Take a bowl and add tofu, season with salt and pepper
2. Set your Foodi to Saute mode and add butter , let it melt
3. Add onions and Saute for 3 minutes
4. Add seasoned tofu and cook for 2 minutes more
5. Add cheddar and gently stir

6. Lock the lid and bring down the Air Crisp mode, let the dish cook on "Air Crisp" mode for 3 minutes at 340 degrees F

7. Once done, take the dish out, serve and enjoy!

Nutrition Values (Per Serving)

- Calories: 184
- Fat: 12g
- Carbohydrates: 5g
- Protein: 12g

The Early Morning Ballet Of Ham And Spinach

(Prepping time: 5 minutes\ Cooking time: 30 minutes |For 6 servings)

Ingredients

- 3 pounds fresh baby spinach
- ½ cup cream
- 28 ounces ham, sliced
- 4 tablespoons butter, melted
- Salt and pepper to taste

Directions

1. Set your Ninja Foodi to Saute mode and add butter, let it melt
2. Add spinach and Saute for 3 minutes
3. Top with cream, ham slices, salt and pepper
4. Lock the Air Fryer lid and let it Bake/Roast for 8 minutes at 360 degrees F
5. Remove the dish from the Foodi and serve
6. Enjoy!

Nutrition Values (Per Serving)

- Calories: 188
- Fat: 12g
- Carbohydrates: 5g
- Protein: 14g

Chapter 3: Healthy Vegetarian And Vegan Recipes

Cheese Dredged Cauliflower Delight

(Prepping time: 5 minutes\ Cooking time: 30 minutes |For 6 servings)

Ingredients

- 1 tablespoon Keto-Friendly mustard
- 1 head cauliflower
- 1 teaspoon avocado mayonnaise
- ½ cup parmesan cheese, grated
- ¼ cup butter, cut into small pieces

Directions

1. Set your Ninja Foodi to Saute mode and add butter, let it melt
2. Add cauliflower and Saute for 3 minutes
3. Add remaining ingredients and lock lid
4. Cook on PRESSURE mode for 30 minutes on HIGH pressure
5. Release pressure natural over 10 minutes
6. Serve and enjoy!

Nutrition Values (Per Serving)

- Calories: 155
- Fat: 13g
- Carbohydrates: 2g
- Protein: 7g

Comfortable Mushroom Soup

(Prepping time: 10 minutes\ Cooking time: 10 minutes |For 6 servings)

Ingredients

- 1 small onion, diced
- 8 ounces white button mushrooms, chopped
- 8 ounces portabella mushrooms
- 2 garlic cloves, minced
- ¼ cup dry white wine vinegar
- 2 and ½ cup mushroom stock
- 2 teaspoons salt
- 1 teaspoon fresh thyme

- ¼ teaspoon black pepper

Cashew Cream

- 1/3 cup of raw cashew
- ½ a cup of mushroom stock

Directions

1. Add onion, mushroom to the pot and set your Ninja Foodi to Saute mode
2. Cook for 8 minutes and stir from time to time
3. Add garlic and Saute for 2 minutes more
4. Add wine and Saute until evaporated
5. Add thyme, pepper, salt, Mushroom stock, and stir
6. Lock up the lid and cook on HIGH pressure for 5 minutes
7. Perform quick release
8. Transfer cashew and water to the blender and blend well
9. Remove lid and transfer mix to the blender
10. Blend until smooth
11. Server and enjoy!

Nutrition Values (Per Serving)

- Calories: 193
- Fats: 12g
- Carbs:15g
- Protein: 5

Chives And Radishes Platter
(Prepping time: 10 minutes\ Cooking time: 7 minutes |For 4 servings)

Ingredients

- 2 cups radishes, quartered
- ½ cup chicken stock
- Salt and pepper to taste
- 2 tablespoons melted ghee
- 1 tablespoon chives, chopped
- 1 tablespoon lemon zest, grated

Direction

1. Add radishes, stock, salt, pepper, zest to your Ninja Foodi and stir
2. Lock lid and cook on HIGH pressure for 7 minutes
3. Quick release pressure

4. Add melted ghee, toss well
5. Sprinkle chives and enjoy!

Nutrition Values (Per Serving)

- Calories: 102
- Fat: 4g
- Carbohydrates: 6g
- Protein: 5g

Garlic And Swiss Chard Garlic

(Prepping time: 10 minutes \ Cooking time: 4 minutes |For 4 servings)

Ingredients

- 2 tablespoons ghee
- 3 tablespoons lemon juice
- ½ cup chicken stock
- 4 bacon slices, chopped
- 1 bunch Swiss chard, chopped
- ½ teaspoon garlic paste
- Salt and pepper to taste

Directions

1. Set your Ninja Foodi to Saute mode and add bacon, stir well and cook for a few minutes
2. Add ghee, lemon juice, garlic paste, and stir
3. Add Swiss chard, salt, pepper, and stock
4. Lock lid and cook on HIGH pressure for 3 minutes
5. Quick release pressure and serve
6. Enjoy!

Nutrition Values (Per Serving)

- Calories: 160
- Fat: 8g
- Carbohydrates: 6g
- Protein: 4g

Healthy Rosemary And Celery Dish

(Prepping time: 10 minutes\ Cooking time: 5 minutes |For 4 servings)

Ingredients

- 1 pound celery, cubed
- 1 cup of water
- 2 garlic cloves, minced
- Salt and pepper
- ¼ teaspoon dry rosemary
- 1 tablespoon olive oil

Direction

1. Add water to your Ninja Foodi and place steamer basket
2. Add celery cubs to basket and lock lid, cook on HIGH pressure for 4 minutes
3. Quick release pressure
4. Take a bowl and add mix in oil, garlic, and rosemary
5. Whisk well
6. Add steamed celery to the bowl and toss well, spread on a lined baking sheet
7. Broil for 3 minutes using the Air Crisping lid at 250 degrees F
8. Serve and enjoy!

Nutrition Values (Per Serving)

- Calories: 100
- Fat: 3g
- Carbohydrates: 8g
- Protein: 3g

Awesome Veggie Hash

(Prepping time: 10 minutes \ Cooking time: 15 minutes |For 4 servings)

Ingredients

- 1 cups cauliflower, chopped
- 1 teaspoon mustard
- ½ cup dark leaf kale, chopped
- 1 tablespoon lemon juice
- ½ cup spinach, chopped
- ½ teaspoon salt
- 2 garlic cloves
- ½ teaspoon pepper
- 6 whole eggs
- 3 teaspoons coconut oil

Directions

1. Set your Ninja Foodi to Saute mode and add coconut oil, add garlic, cook until fragrant
2. Add chopped cauliflower and cook for 5 minutes
3. Stir in all ingredients except eggs, cook for 2 minutes
4. Stir in eggs, lock lid and cook for 2 minutes on HIGH pressure
5. Quick release pressure
6. Enjoy!

Nutrition Values (Per Serving)

- Calories: 480
- Fat: 35g
- Carbohydrates: 8g
- Protein: 22g

Thyme And Carrot Dish With Dill
(Prepping time: 5 minutes\ Cooking time: 5 minutes |For 4 servings)

Ingredients

- ½ cup of water
- 1 pound baby carrots
- 3 tablespoons stevia
- 1 tablespoon thyme, chopped
- 1 tablespoon dill, chopped
- Salt and pepper to taste
- 2 tablespoons ghee

Direction

1. Add trivet to your Ninja Foodi, add carrots and add water
2. Lock lid and cook on HIGH pressure for 3 minutes
3. Quick release pressure
4. Drain and transfer to a bowl
5. Set your Ninja Foodi to Saute mode and add ghee, let it melt
6. Add stevia, thyme dill, and carrots
7. Stir well for a few minutes
8. Serve and enjoy!

Nutrition Values (Per Serving)

- Calories: 162
- Fat: 4g
- Carbohydrates: 8g
- Protein: 3g

Creative Coconut Cabbage

(Prepping time: 10 minutes \ Cooking time: 7 minutes |For 4 servings)

Ingredients

- 2 tablespoons lemon juice
- 1/3 medium carrot, sliced
- ½ ounces, yellow onion, sliced
- 1/2 cup cabbage, shredded
- 1 teaspoon turmeric powder
- 1 ounce dry coconut
- ½ tablespoon mustard powder
- ½ teaspoon mild curry powder
- 1 large garlic cloves, diced
- 1 and ½ teaspoons salt
- 1/3 cup water
- 3 tablespoons olive oil
- 3 large whole eggs
- 3 large egg yolks

Directions

1. Set your Ninja Foodi to Saute mode and add oil, stir in onions, salt and cook for 4 minutes
2. Stir in spices, garlic and Saute for 30 seconds
3. Stir in rest of the ingredients, lock lid and cook on HIGH pressure for 3 minutes
4. Naturally, release pressure over 10 minutes
5. Serve and enjoy!

Nutrition Values (Per Serving)

- Calories: 400
- Fat: 34g
- Carbohydrates: 10g
- Protein: 14g

Complete Cauliflower Zoodles

(Prepping time: 10 minutes\ Cooking time: 8 minutes |For 6 servings)

Ingredients

- 2 tablespoons butter

- 2 cloves garlic
- 7-8 cauliflower florets
- 1 cup vegetable broth
- 2 teaspoons salt
- 2 cups spinach, coarsely chopped
- 2 green onions, chopped
- 1 pound of zoodles (Spiralized Zucchini)

Garnish

- Chopped sun-dried tomatoes
- Balsamic vinegar
- Gorgonzola cheese

Directions

1. Set your Ninja Foodi to Saute mode and add butter, allow the butter to melt
2. Add garlic cloves and Saute for 2 minutes
3. Add cauliflower, broth, salt and lock up the lid and cook on HIGH pressure for 6 minutes
4. Prepare the zoodles
5. Perform a naturally release over 10 minutes
6. Use an immersion blender to blend the mixture in the pot to a puree
7. Pour the sauce over the zoodles
8. Serve with a garnish of cheese, sun-dried tomatoes and a drizzle of balsamic vinegar
9. Enjoy!

Nutrition Values (Per Serving)

- Calories: 78
- Fats: 5g
- Carbs 0.6g
- Protein:8g

Simple Mushroom Hats And Eggs
(Prepping time: 10 minutes\ Cooking time: 9 minutes |For 1 serving)

Ingredients

- 4 ounces mushroom hats
- 1 teaspoon butter, melted
- 4 quail eggs
- ½ teaspoon ground black pepper
- ¼ teaspoon salt

Directions

1. Spread the mushroom hats with the butter inside
2. Then beat the eggs into mushroom hats
3. Sprinkle with salt and ground black pepper
4. Transfer the mushroom hats on the rack
5. Lower the air fryer lid
6. Cook the meat for 7 minutes at 365 F
7. Check the mushroom, if it is not cooked fully then cook them for 2 minutes more
8. Serve and enjoy!

Nutrition Values (Per Serving)

- Calories: 118
- Fat: 8.2g
- Carbohydrates: 4.6g
- Protein: 8.4g

Ginger And Butternut Bisque Yum

(Prepping time: 10 minutes\ Cooking time: 8 minutes |For 6 servings)

Ingredients

- 1 cup of diced yellow onion
- 4 minced cloves of garlic
- 2 teaspoon of peeled and chopped ginger
- 1 cup of chopped carrot
- 1 green apple chopped
- 1 peeled and chopped butternut squash
- 1 teaspoon salt
- 2 cups of water
- ¼ cup of finely chopped parsley
- Black pepper

Directions

1. Prepare the ingredients accordingly and keep them on the side
2. Set your Ninja Foodie to Saute mode and add onions, cook for minutes
3. Add just a splash of water
4. Add garlic, carrot, ginger, apple, squash, and salt
5. Give it a nice stir
6. Add water and lock up the lid
7. Cook on HIGH pressure for 5 minutes

8. Naturally, release the pressure

9. Allow it to cool for 15 minutes

10. Blend the soup in batches, or you may use an immersion blender as well to blend in the pot until it is creamy

11. Add parsley and season with some black pepper

12. Serve and enjoy!

Nutrition Values (Per Serving)

- Protein: 3g
- Carbs: 14g
- Fats: 5g
- Calories: 116

Garlic And Dill Carrot Fiesta

(Prepping time: 5 minutes\ Cooking time: 12 minutes |For 4 servings)

Ingredients

- 3 cups carrots, chopped
- 1 tablespoon melted butter
- ½ teaspoon garlic sea salt
- 1 tablespoon fresh dill, minced
- 1 cup water

Directions

1. Add listed ingredients to Ninja Foodi

2. Stir and lock lid, cook on HIGH pressure for 10 minutes

3. Release pressure naturally over 10 minutes

4. Quick release pressure and remove lid

5. Serve with a topping of dill, enjoy!

Nutrition Values (Per Serving)

- Calories: 207
- Fat: 16g
- Carbohydrates: 5g
- Protein: 8g

Cool Indian Palak Paneer

(Prepping time: 10 minutes\ Cooking time: 5 minutes |For 4 servings)

Ingredients

- 2 teaspoons olive oil
- 5 garlic cloves, chopped
- 1 tablespoon fresh ginger, chopped
- 1 large yellow onion, chopped
- ½ jalapeno chile, chopped
- 1 pound fresh spinach
- 2 tomatoes, chopped
- 2 teaspoons ground cumin
- ½ teaspoon cayenne
- 2 teaspoons Garam masala
- 1 teaspoon ground turmeric
- 1 teaspoon salt
- ½ cup water
- 1 and ½ cup paneer cubes
- ½ cup heavy whip cream

Directions

1. Pre-heat your Ninja Foodi using Saute mode on HIGH heat, once the pot is hot, add oil and let it shimmer

2. Add garlic, ginger and chile, Saute for 2-3 minutes

3. Add onion, spinach, tomatoes, cumin, cayenne, garam masala, turmeric, salt and water

4. Lock lid and cook on HIGH pressure for 2 minutes

5. Release pressure naturally over 10 minutes

6. Use an immersion blender to puree the mixture to your desired consistency

7. Gently stir in paneer and top with a drizzle of cream. Enjoy!

Nutrition Values (Per Serving)

- Calories: 185
- Fat: 14g
- Carbohydrates: 7g
- Protein: 7g

Astounding Caramelized Onions

(Prepping time: 10 minutes\ Cooking time: 45 minutes |For 4 servings)

Ingredients

- 2 tablespoons unsalted butter
- 3 large onions, sliced
- 2 tablespoons water

- 1 teaspoon salt

Directions

1. Set your pot to Saute mode and adjust the heat to Medium, pre-heat the inner pot for 5 minutes
2. Add butter and let it melt, add onions, water , salt, and stir well
3. Lock pressure lid into place, making sure that the pressure valve is locked
4. Cook on HIGH pressure for 30 minutes
5. Quick release the pressure once done
6. Remove the lid and set the pot to Saute mode, let it sear in the Medium-HIGH mode for about 15 minutes until the liquid is almost gone
7. Enjoy!

Nutrition Values (Per Serving)

- Calories: 110
- Fat: 6g
- Carbohydrates: 10g
- Protein: 2g

Special Lunch-Worthy Green Beans
(Prepping time: 5 minutes\ Cooking time: 10 minutes |For 4 servings)

Ingredients

- 2-3 pounds fresh green beans
- 2 tablespoons butter
- 1 garlic clove, minced
- Salt and pepper to taste
- 1 and ½ cups water

Directions

1. Add all listed ingredients to your Ninja Foodi pot
2. Lock lid and cook on HIGH pressure for 5 minutes
3. Release pressure quickly and serve
4. Enjoy!

Nutrition Values (Per Serving)

- Calories: 87
- Fat: 6g
- Carbohydrates: 7g

- Protein: 3g

Healthy Cauliflower Mash

(Prepping time: 10 minutes\ Cooking time: 5 minutes |For 4 servings)

Ingredients

- 1 tablespoon butter, soft
- ½ cup feta cheese
- Salt and pepper to taste
- 1 large head cauliflower, chopped into large pieces
- 1 garlic cloves, minced
- 2 teaspoons fresh chives, minced

Directions

1. Add the pot to your Ninja Foodi and add water
2. Add steamer basket on top and add cauliflower pieces
3. Lock lid and cook on HIGH pressure for 5 minutes
4. Quick release pressure
5. Open lid and use an immersion blender to mash the cauliflower
6. Blend until you have your desired consistency and enjoy!

Nutrition Values (Per Serving)

- Calories: 124
- Fat: 10g
- Carbohydrates: 5g
- Protein: 5g

Beets And Greens With Cool Horseradish Sauce

(Prepping time: 5 minutes\ Cooking time: 10-15 minutes |For 4 servings)

Ingredients

- 2 large beets with greens, scrubbed and root ends trimmed
- 1 cup water, for steaming
- 2 tablespoons sour cream
- 1 tablespoon almond milk
- 1 teaspoon prepared horseradish
- ¼ teaspoon lemon zest
- 1/8 teaspoon salt
- 2 teaspoon unsalted butter

- 1 tablespoon minced fresh chives

Directions

1. Trim off beet greens and keep them on the side
2. Add water to the Ninja Foodi and place steamer basket, place beets in steamer basket
3. Lock lid and cook on HIGH pressure for 10 minutes, release pressure naturally over 10 minutes
4. While the beets are being cooked, wash greens and slice them into ½ inch thick ribbons
5. Take a bowl and whisk in sour cream, horseradish, lemon zest, 1/16 teaspoon of salt
6. Once the cooking is done, remove lid and remove beets, let them cool
7. Use a pairing knife to peel them and slice them into large bite-sized pieces
8. Remove steamer from the Ninja Foodi and pour out water
9. Set your Foodi to "Saute" mode and add butter, let it melt
10. Once the butter stops foaming, add beet greens sprinkle remaining 1/6 teaspoon salt and cook for 3-4 minutes
11. Return beets to the Foodi and heat for 1-2 minutes, stirring
12. Transfer beets and greens to platter and drizzle sour cream mixture
13. Sprinkle chives and serve. Enjoy!

Nutrition Values (Per Serving)

- Calories: 70
- Fat: 4g
- Carbohydrates: 9g
- Protein: 2g

Summertime Veggie Soup

(Prepping time: 10 minutes\ Cooking time: 3 minutes |For 6 servings)

Ingredients

- 3 cups leeks, sliced
- 6 cups rainbow chard, stems and leaves, chopped
- 1 cup celery, chopped
- 2 tablespoons garlic, minced
- 1 teaspoon dried oregano
- 1 teaspoon salt
- 2 teaspoons fresh ground black pepper
- 3 cups chicken broth
- 2 cups yellow summer squash, sliced into 1/ inch slices
- ¼ cup fresh parsley, chopped
- ¾ cup heavy whip cream

- 4-6 tablespoons parmesan cheese, grated

Directions

1. Add leeks, chard, celery, 1 tablespoon garlic, oregano, salt, pepper and broth to your Ninja Foodi
2. Lock lid and cook on HIGH pressure for 3 minutes
3. Quick release pressure
4. Open lid and add more broth, set your pot to Saute mode and adjust heat to HIGH
5. Add yellow squash, parsley and remaining 1 tablespoon garlic
6. Let it cook for 2-3 minutes until the squash is soft
7. Stir in cream and sprinkle parmesan
8. Serve and enjoy!

Nutrition Values (Per Serving)

- Calories: 210
- Fat: 14g
- Carbohydrates: 10g
- Protein: 10g

Delicious Mushroom Stroganoff

(Prepping time: 5 minutes\ Cooking time: 10 minutes |For 6 servings)

Ingredients

- ¼ cup unsalted butter, cubed
- 1 pound cremini mushrooms, halved
- 1 large onion, halved
- 4 garlic cloves, minced
- 2 cups vegetable broth
- ½ teaspoon salt
- ¼ teaspoon fresh black pepper
- 1 and ½ cups sour cream
- ¼ cup fresh flat-leaf parsley, chopped
- 1 cup grated parmesan cheese

Directions

1. Add butter, mushrooms, onion, garlic, vegetable broth, salt, pepper and paprika
2. Gently stir and lock lid
3. Cook on HIGH pressure for 5 minutes
4. Release pressure naturally over 10 minutes
5. Serve by stirring in sour cream and with a garnish of parsley and parmesan cheese

6. Enjoy!

Nutrition Values (Per Serving)

- Calories: 453
- Fat: 37g
- Carbohydrates: 11g
- Protein: 19g

Everyday Use Veggie-Stock

(Prepping time: 10 minutes\ Cooking time: 100 minutes |For 1 quart)

Ingredients

- 1 onion, quartered
- 2 large carrots, peeled and cut into 1 inch pieces
- 1 tablespoon olive oil
- 12 ounces mushrooms, sliced
- ¼ teaspoon salt
- 3 and ½ cups water

Directions

1. Take cook and crisp basket out of the inner pot, close crisping lid and let it pre-heat for 3 minutes at 400 degrees F on Bake/Roast settings
2. While the pot heats up, add onion, carrot chunks in the Cook and Crisp basket and drizzle vegetable oil, toss well
3. Place basket back into the inner pot, close crisping lid and cook for 15 minutes at 400 degrees F on Bake/Roast mode
4. Make sure to shake the basket halfway through
5. Remove basket from pot and add onions, carrots, mushrooms, water and season with salt
6. Lock pressure lid and seal the valves, cook on HIGH pressure for 60 minutes
7. Release the pressure naturally over 10 minutes
8. Line a colander with cheesecloth and place it over a large bowl, pour vegetables and stock into the colander
9. Strain the stock and discard veggies
10. Enjoy and use as needed!

Nutrition Values (Per Serving)

- Calories: 45
- Fat: 4g

- Carbohydrates: 3g
- Protein: 0g

Groovy Broccoli Florets

(Prepping time: 10 minutes\ Cooking time: 6 minutes |For 4 servings)

Ingredients

- 4 tablespoons butter, melted
- Salt and pepper to taste
- 2 pounds broccoli florets
- 1 cup whipping cream

Directions

1. Place a steamer basket in your Ninja Foodi (bottom part) and add water
2. Place florets on top of the basket and lock lid
3. Cook on HIGH pressure for 5 minutes
4. Quick release pressure
5. Transfer florets from the steamer basket to the pot
6. Add salt, pepper, butter and stir
7. Lock crisping lid and cook on Air Crisp mode for 360 degrees F
8. Serve and enjoy!

Nutrition Values (Per Serving)

- Calories: 178
- Fat: 14g
- Carbohydrates: 8g
- Protein: 5g

Offbeat Cauliflower And Cheddar Soup

(Prepping time: 10 minutes\ Cooking time: 5 minutes |For 8 servings)

Ingredients

- ¼ cup butter
- ½ sweet onion, chopped
- 1 head cauliflower, chopped
- 4 cups herbed vegetable stock
- ½ teaspoon ground nutmeg
- 1 cup heavy whip cream
- Salt and pepper as needed
- 1 cup cheddar cheese, shredded

Directions

1. Set your Ninja Foodi to sauté mode and add butter , let it heat up and melt
2. Add onion and Cauliflower, Saute for 10 minutes until tender and lightly browned
3. Add vegetable stock and nutmeg, bring to a boil
4. Lock lid and cook on HIGH pressure for 5 minutes, quick release pressure once done
5. Remove pot and from Foodi and stir in heavy cream, puree using immersion blender
6. Season with more salt and pepper and serve with a topping of cheddar
7. Enjoy!

Nutrition Values (Per Serving)

- Calories: 227
- Fat: 21g
- Carbohydrates: 4g
- Protein: 8g

Powerful Medi-Cheese Spinach

(Prepping time: 5 minutes\ Cooking time: 15 minutes |For 4 servings)

Ingredients

- 4 tablespoons butter
- 2 pounds spinach, chopped and boiled
- Salt and pepper to taste
- 2/3 cup Kalamata olives, halved and pitted
- 1 and ½ cups feta cheese, grated
- 4 teaspoons fresh lemon zest, grated

Directions

1. Take a bowl and mix spinach, butter, salt, pepper and transfer the mixture to your Crisping Basket of the Ninja Foodi
2. Transfer basket to your Foodi and lock Crisping lid
3. Cook for 15 minutes on Air Crisp mode on 340 degrees F
4. Serve by stirring in olives, lemon zest and feta
5. Enjoy!

Nutrition Values (Per Serving)

- Calories: 274
- Fat: 18g
- Carbohydrates: 6g
- Protein: 10g

Awesome Butternut Squash Soup

(Prepping time: 10 minutes\ Cooking time: 16 minutes |For 4 servings)

Ingredients

- 1 and ½ pounds butternut squash, baked, peeled and cubed
- ½ cup green onions, chopped
- 3 tablespoons butter
- ½ cup carrots, peeled and chopped
- ½ cup celery, chopped
- 29 ounces vegetable stock
- 1 garlic clove, peeled and minced
- ½ teaspoon Italian seasoning
- 15 ounces canned tomatoes, diced
- Salt and pepper to taste
- 1/8 teaspoon red pepper flakes
- 1/8 teaspoon nutmeg, grated
- 1 and ½ cup half and half

Directions

1. Set your Ninja Foodi to "Saute" mode and add butter, let it melt
2. Add celery, carrots, onion and stir cook for 3 minutes
3. Add garlic, stir cook for 1 minute
4. Add squash, tomatoes, stock, Italian seasoning, salt, pepper, pepper flakes and nutmeg, stir
5. Lock lid and cook on HIGH pressure for 10 minutes
6. Release pressure naturally over 10 minutes
7. Use an immersion blender to puree the mix
8. Set the food to Saute mode on LOW and add half and half, stir cook for 1-2 minutes until thickened
9. Divide and serve with a sprinkle of green onions on top
10. Enjoy!

Nutrition Values (Per Serving)

- Calories: 250
- Fat: 22g
- Carbohydrates: 8g
- Protein: 3g

Chapter 4: Flavorful Chicken And Poultry Recipes

Juicy Sesame Garlic Chicken Wings

(Prepping time: 10 minutes\ Cooking time: 25 minutes |For 4 servings)

Ingredients

- 24 chicken wing segments
- 2 tablespoons toasted sesame oil
- 2 tablespoons Asian-Chile-Garlic sauce
- 2 tablespoons stevia
- 2 garlic cloves, minced
- 1 tablespoon toasted sesame seeds

Directions

1. Add 1 cup water to Foodi's inner pot, place reversible rack in the pot in lower portions, place chicken wings in the rack
2. Place lid into place and seal the valve
3. Select pressure mode to HIGH and cook for 10 minutes
4. Make the glaze by taking a large bowl and whisking in sesame oil, Chile-Garlic sauce, honey and garlic
5. Once the chicken is cooked, quick release the pressure and remove pressure lid
6. Remove rack from the pot and empty remaining water
7. Return inner pot to the base
8. Cover with crisping lid and select Air Crisp mode, adjust the temperature to 375 degrees F, pre-heat for 3 minutes
9. While the Foodi pre-heats, add wings to the sauce and toss well to coat it
10. Transfer wings to the basket, leaving any excess sauce in the bowl
11. Place the basket in Foodi and close with Crisping mode, select Air Crisp mode and let it cook for 8 minutes, gently toss the wings and let it cook for 8 minutes more
12. Once done, drizzle any sauce and sprinkle sesame seeds
13. Enjoy!

Nutrition Values (Per Serving)

- Calories: 440
- Fat: 32g
- Carbohydrates: 12g
- Protein: 28g

Lemon And Chicken Extravaganza

(Prepping time: 5 minutes\ Cooking time: 18 minutes |For 4 servings)

Ingredients

- 4 bone-in, skin on chicken thighs
- Salt and pepper to taste
- 2 tablespoons butter, divided
- 2 teaspoons garlic, minced
- ½ cup herbed chicken stock
- ½ cup heavy whip cream
- ½ a lemon, juiced

Directions

1. Season your chicken thighs generously with salt and pepper
2. Set your Foodi to sauté mode and add oil, let it heat up
3. Add thigh, Sauté both sides for 6 minutes
4. Remove thigh to a platter and keep it on the side
5. Add garlic, cook for 2 minutes
6. Whisk in chicken stock, heavy cream, lemon juice and gently stir
7. Bring the mix to a simmer and reintroduce chicken
8. Lock lid and cook for 10 minutes on HIGH pressure
9. Release pressure over 10 minutes
10. Serve and enjoy!

Nutrition Values (Per Serving)

- Calories: 294
- Fat: 26g
- Carbohydrates: 4g
- Protein: 12g

Bruschetta Chicken Meal

(Prepping time: 5 minutes\ Cooking time: 9 minutes |For 4 servings)

Ingredients

- 2 tablespoons balsamic vinegar
- 1/3 cup olive oil

- 2 teaspoons garlic cloves, minced
- 1 teaspoon black pepper
- ½ teaspoon salt
- ½ cup sun-dried tomatoes, in olive oil
- 2 pounds chicken breasts, quartered, boneless
- 2 tablespoons fresh basil, chopped

Direction

1. Take a bowl and whisk in vinegar, oil, garlic, pepper, salt
2. Fold in tomatoes, basil and add breast, mix well
3. Transfer to fridge and let it sit for 30 minutes
4. Add everything to Ninja Foodi and lock lid, cook on High Pressure for 9 minutes
5. Quick release pressure
6. Serve and enjoy!

Nutrition Values (Per Serving)

- Calories: 480
- Fat: 26g
- Carbohydrates: 4g
- Protein: 52g

The Great Hainanese Chicken

(Prepping time: 20 minutes \ Cooking time: 4 hours |For 4 servings)

Ingredients

- 1 ounces ginger, peeled
- 6 garlic cloves, crushed
- 6 bundles cilantro/basil leaves
- 1 teaspoon salt
- 1 tablespoon sesame oil
- 3 (1 and ½ pounds each) chicken meat, ready to cook

For Dip

- 2 tablespoons ginger, minced
- 1 teaspoon garlic, minced
- 1 tablespoon chicken stock
- 1 teaspoon sesame oil
- ½ teaspoon sugar
- Salt to taste

Directions

1. Add chicken, garlic, ginger, leaves, and salt in your Ninja Food
2. Add enough water to fully submerge chicken, lock lid cook on SLOW COOK mode on LOW for 4 hours
3. Release pressure naturally
4. Take chicken out of pot and chill for 10 minutes
5. Take a bowl and add all the dipping ingredients and blend well in a food processor
6. Take chicken out of ice bath and drain, chop into serving pieces
7. Arrange onto a serving platter
8. Brush chicken with sesame oil
9. Serve with ginger dip
10. Enjoy!

Nutrition Values (Per Serving)

- Calories: 535
- Fat: 45g
- Carbohydrates: 5g
- Protein: 28g

A Genuine Hassel Back Chicken

(Prepping time: 5 minutes\ Cooking time: 60 minutes |For 4 servings)

Ingredients

- 4 tablespoons butter
- Salt and pepper to taste
- 2 cups fresh mozzarella cheese, thinly sliced
- 8 large chicken breasts
- 4 large Roma tomatoes, thinly sliced

Directions

1. Make few deep slits in chicken breasts, season with salt and pepper
2. Stuff mozzarella cheese slices and tomatoes in chicken slits
3. Grease Ninja Foodi pot with butter and arrange stuffed chicken breasts
4. Lock lid and BAKE/ROAST for 1 hour at 365 degrees F
5. Serve and enjoy!

Nutrition Values (Per Serving)

- Calories: 278
- Fat: 15g

- Carbohydrates: 3.8g
- Protein: 15g

Shredded Up Salsa Chicken

(Prepping time: 5 minutes\ Cooking time: 20 minutes |For 4 servings)

Ingredients

- 1 pound chicken breast, skin and bones removed
- ¾ teaspoon cumin
- ½ teaspoon salt
- Pinch of oregano
- Pepper to taste
- 1 cup chunky salsa Keto friendly

Directions

1. Season chicken with spices and add to Ninja Foodi
2. Cover with salsa and lock lid, cook on HIGH pressure for 20 minutes
3. Quick release pressure
4. Add chicken to a platter and shred the chicken
5. Serve and enjoy!

Nutrition Values (Per Serving)

- Calories: 125
- Fat: 3g
- Carbohydrates: 2g
- Protein: 22g

Mexico's Favorite Chicken Soup

(Prepping time: 5 minutes\ Cooking time: 20 minutes |For 4 servings)

Ingredients

- 2 cups chicken, shredded
- 4 tablespoons olive oil
- ½ cup cilantro, chopped
- 8 cups chicken broth
- 1/3 cup salsa

- 1 teaspoon onion powder
- ½ cup scallions, chopped
- 4 ounces green chilies, chopped
- ½ teaspoon habanero, minced
- 1 cup celery root, chopped
- 1 teaspoon cumin
- 1 teaspoon garlic powder
- Salt and pepper to taste

Directions

1. Add all ingredients to Ninja Foodi
2. Stir and lock lid, cook on HIGH pressure for 10 minutes
3. Release pressure naturally over 10 minutes
4. Serve and enjoy!

Nutrition Values (Per Serving)

- Calories: 204
- Fat: 14g
- Carbohydrates: 4g
- Protein: 14g

Taiwanese Chicken Delight
(Prepping time: 5 minutes\ Cooking time: 10 minutes |For 4 servings)

Ingredients

- 6 dried red chilis
- ¼ cup sesame oil
- 2 tablespoons ginger
- ¼ cup garlic, minced
- ¼ cup red wine vinegar
- ¼ cup coconut aminos
- Salt as needed
- 1.2 teaspoon xanthan gum (for the finish)
- ¼ cup Thai basil, chopped

Directions

1. Set your Ninja Foodi to Saute mode and add ginger, chilis, garlic and Saute for 2 minutes
2. Add remaining ingredients
3. Lock lid and cook on HIGH pressure for 10 minutes

4. Quick release pressure
5. Serve and enjoy!

Nutrition Values (Per Serving)

- Calories: 307
- Fat: 15g
- Carbohydrates: 7g
- Protein: 31g

Cabbage And Chicken Meatballs

(Prepping time: 10 minutes + 30 minutes\ Cooking time: 4-6 minutes |For 4 servings)

Ingredients

- 1 pound ground chicken
- ¼ cup heavy whip cream
- 2 teaspoons salt
- ½ teaspoon ground caraway seeds
- 1 and ½ teaspoons fresh ground black pepper, divided
- 1/4 teaspoon ground allspice
- 4-6 cups green cabbage, thickly chopped
- ½ cup almond milk
- 2 tablespoons unsalted butter

Directions

1. Transfer meat to a bowl and add cream, 1 teaspoon salt, caraway, ½ teaspoon pepper, allspice and mix it well
2. Let the mixture chill for 30 minutes
3. Once the mixture is ready, use your hands to scoop the mixture into meatballs
4. Add half of your balls to Ninja Foodi pot and cover with half of the cabbage
5. Add remaining balls and cover with rest of the cabbage
6. Add milk, pats of butter, season with salt and pepper
7. Lock lid and cook on HIGH pressure for 4 minutes
8. Quick release pressure
9. Unlock lid and serve
10. Enjoy!

Nutrition Values (Per Serving)

- Calories: 294

- Fat: 26g
- Carbohydrates: 4g
- Protein: 12g

Perfectly Braised Chicken Thigh With Chokeful Of Mushrooms

(Prepping time: 10 minutes\ Cooking time: 30 minutes |For 4 servings)

Ingredients

- 4 chicken thigh, bone in- skin on
- 1 teaspoon salt
- 1 tablespoon olive oil
- ½ small onion, sliced
- ½ cup white wine vinegar
- ½ cup chicken stock
- 1 cup frozen artichoke hearts, thawed and drained
- 1 bay leaf
- Fresh ground black pepper
- ¼ cup heavy cream

Directions

1. Set your Foodi to Sauté mode and set it to Medium-HIGH, pre-heat for 5 minutes
2. Pour olive oil and wait until it shimmers
3. Add chicken thighs, skin side-side down, cook for 4-5 minutes
4. Turn and sear the other side for 1 minute
5. Remove from pot
6. Add onion, sprinkle with remaining salt, cook for 2 minutes more until tender
7. Add wine and bring to a boil. Cook for 2-3 minutes, until reduced by half
8. Add chicken stock, artichoke hearts, bay leaf, thyme, several grinds of pepper, stir well
9. Place chicken thigh back to the pot (skin side up), lock pressure lid into place and seal the valve
10. Select pressure mode to HIGH and cook for 5 minutes
11. Once done, quick release pressure
12. use tongs to transfer chicken to Reversible Rack in the upper position, add mushrooms to sauce and stir. Set rack in the pot
13. Close with crisping lid and select Bake/Roast, adjust the temperature to 375 degrees F, cook for 12 minutes
14. Once done, open lid and transfer chicken to the platter, add heavy cream and stir into the sauce. stir in sauce, season with salt and pepper
15. Pour sauce and vegetables around chicken, serve and enjoy!

Nutrition Values (Per Serving)

- Calories: 268
- Fat: 20g
- Carbohydrates: 7g
- Protein: 19g

Lemon And Butter Chicken Extravagant

(Prepping time: 10 minutes\ Cooking time: 10 minutes |For 4 servings)

Ingredients

- 4 bone-in, skin on chicken thighs
- salt and pepper as needed
- 2 tablespoons butter, divided
- 2 teaspoons garlic, minced
- 1/2 cup herbed chicken stock
- 1/2 cup heavy whip cream
- 1/2 a lemon, juiced

Directions

1. Season chicken thighs with salt and pepper
2. Set your Ninja Foodi to Sauté mode and add oil, let it heat up
3. Add chicken thighs and saute both sides until golden, total for 6 minutes
4. Remove thighs to a plater and keep it on the side
5. Add garlic and cook for 2 minutes
6. Whisk in chicken stock, heavy cream, lemon juice and stir, bring the sauce to simmer and reintroduce the chicken
7. Lock lid and cook for 10 minutes on HIGH pressure
8. Release pressure naturally over 10 minutes
9. Serve warm and enjoy!

Nutrition Values (Per Serving)
- Calories: 294
- Fat: 26g
- Carbohydrates: 4g
- Protein: 12g

Creative Cabbage And Chicken Meatball

(Prepping time: 15 minutes\ Cooking time: 4 minutes |For 4 servings)

Ingredients

- 1 pound ground chicken
- 1/4 cup heavy whip cream
- 2 teaspoon salt
- 1/2 teaspoon ground caraway seeds
- 1 and 1/2 teaspoons fresh ground black pepper, divided
- 1/4 teaspoon ground allspice
- 4-6 cups green cabbage, thickly chopped
- 1/2 cup almond milk
- 2 tablespoons unsalted butter

Directions

1. Transfer meat to a bowl
2. Add cream, 1 teaspoon salt, caraway, 1/2 teaspoon pepper, allspice and mix well
3. Refrigerate the mixture for 30 minutes
4. Once the mixture is cool, use your hands to scoop the mixture into meatballs
5. Place half of the balls to your Ninja Foodi pot and cover with half of cabbage
6. Add remaining balls and cover with remaining cabbage
7. Add milk, pats of butter and sprinkle 1 teaspoon salt, 1 teaspoon pepper
8. Lock lid and cook on HIGH pressure for 4 minutes
9. Quick release pressure
10. Unlock lid and serve
11. Enjoy!

Nutrition Values (Per Serving)

- Calories: 338
- Fat: 23g
- Carbohydrates: 7g
- Protein: 23g

Spicy Hot Paprika Chicken

(Prepping time: 10 minutes\ Cooking time: 5 minutes |For 4 servings)

Ingredients

- 4 pieces (4 ounces each) chicken breast, skin on
- Salt and pepper as needed
- 1 tablespoon olive oil
- ½ cup sweet onion, chopped
- ½ cup heavy whip cream
- 2 teaspoons smoked paprika
- ½ cup sour cream

- 2 tablespoons fresh parsley, chopped

Directions

1. Lightly season the chicken with salt and pepper
2. Set your Ninja Foodi to Sauté mode and add oil, let the oil heat up
3. Add chicken and sear both sides until properly browned, should take about 15 minutes
4. Remove chicken and transfer them to a plate
5. Take a skillet and place it over medium heat, add onion and Saute for 4 minutes until tender
6. Stir in cream, paprika and bring the liquid simmer
7. Return chicken to the skillet and alongside any juices
8. Transfer the whole mixture to your Ninja Foodi and lock lid, cook on HIGH pressure for 5 minutes
9. Release pressure naturally over 10 minutes
10. Stir in sour cream, serve and enjoy!

Nutrition Values (Per Serving)
- Calories: 389
- Fat: 30g
- Carbohydrates: 4g
- Protein: 25g

Elegant Chicken Stock

(Prepping time: 10 minutes\ Cooking time: 2hours |For 4 servings)

Ingredients

- 2 pounds meaty chicken bones
- ¼ teaspoon salt
- 3 and ½ cups water

Directions

1. Place chicken parts in Foodi and season with salt
2. Add water, place the pressure cooker lid and seal the valve, cook on HIGH pressure for 90 minutes
3. Release the pressure naturally over 10 minutes
4. Line a colander with cheesecloth and place it over a large bowl, pour chicken parts and stock into the colander and strain out the chicken and bones
5. Let the stock cool and let it peel off any layer of fat that might accumulate on the surface
6. Use as needed!

Nutrition Values (Per Serving)
- Calories: 51
- Fat: 3g
- Carbohydrates: 1g
- Protein: 6g

Hot Turkey Cutlets

(Prepping time: 10 minutes\ Cooking time: 15 minutes |For 4 servings)

Ingredients

- 1 teaspoon Greek seasoning
- 1 pound turkey cutlets
- 2 tablespoons olive oil
- 1 teaspoon turmeric powder
- ½ cup almond flour

Directions

1. Take a bowl and add Greek seasoning, turmeric powder, almond flour and mix well
2. Dredge turkey cutlets in the bowl and let it sit for 30 minutes
3. Set your Ninja Foodi to Sauté mode and add oil, let it heat up
4. Add cutlets and Sauté for 2 minutes
5. Lock lid and cook on Low-Medium Pressure for 20 minutes
6. Release pressure naturally over 10 minutes
7. Take the dish out, serve and enjoy!

Nutrition Values (Per Serving)

- Calories: 340
- Fat: 19g
- Carbohydrates: 3.7g
- Protein: 36g

Pulled Up Keto Friendly Chicken Tortilla's

(Prepping time: 15 minutes\ Cooking time: 15 minutes |For 4 servings)

Ingredients

- 1 tablespoon avocado oil
- 1 pound pastured organic boneless chicken breasts
- ½ cup orange juice
- 2 teaspoons gluten-free Worcestershire sauce
- 1 teaspoon garlic powder
- 1 teaspoon salt
- ½ teaspoon chili powder
- ½ teaspoon paprika

Directions

1. Set your Ninja Foodi to Sauté mode and add oil, let the oil heat up
2. Add chicken on top, take a bowl and add remaining ingredients mix well
3. Pour the mixture over chicken
4. Lock lid and cook on HIGH pressure for 15 minutes
5. Release pressure naturally over 10 minutes
6. Shred the chicken and serve over salad green shell such as cabbage or lettuce
7. Enjoy!

Nutrition Values (Per Serving)

- Calories: 338
- Fat: 23g
- Carbohydrates: 10g
- Protein: 23g

Fully-Stuffed Whole Chicken

(Prepping time: 10 minutes\ Cooking time: 8 hours |For 6 servings)

Ingredients

- 1 cup mozzarella cheese
- 4 whole garlic cloves, peeled
- 1 whole chicken (2 pounds), cleaned and pat dried
- Salt and pepper as needed
- 2 tablespoons fresh lemon juice

Directions

1. Stuff the chicken cavity with garlic cloves and mozzarella cheese
2. Season chicken generously with salt and pepper
3. Transfer chicken to your Ninja Foodi and drizzle lemon juice
4. Lock lid and set to "Slow Cooker" mode, let it cook on LOW for 8 hours
5. Once doe, serve and enjoy!

Nutrition Values (Per Serving)

- Calories: 309
- Fat: 12g
- Carbohydrates: 1.6g
- Protein: 45g

Ham-Stuffed Generous Turkey Rolls

(Prepping time: 10 minutes\ Cooking time: 20 minutes |For 8 servings)

Ingredients

- 4 tablespoons fresh sage leaves
- 8 ham slices
- 8 (6 ounces each) turkey cutlets
- Salt and pepper to taste
- 2 tablespoons butter, melted

Directions

1. Season turkey cutlets with salt and pepper
2. Roll turkey cutlets and wrap each of them with ham slices tightly
3. Coat each roll with butter and gently place sage leaves evenly over each cutlet
4. Transfer them to your Ninja Foodi
5. Lock lid and select the "Bake/Roast" mode, bake for 10 minutes a 360 degrees F
6. Open the lid and gently give it a flip, lock lid again and bake for 10 minutes more
7. Once done, serve and enjoy!

Nutrition Values (Per Serving)

- Calories: 467
- Fat: 24g
- Carbohydrates: 1.7g
- Protein: 56g

Sensational Lime And Chicken Chili

(Prepping time: 10 minutes\ Cooking time: 23 minutes |For 6 servings)

Ingredients

- ¼ cup cooking wine (Keto-Friendly)
- ½ cup organic chicken broth
- 1 onion, diced
- 1 teaspoon salt
- ½ teaspoon paprika
- 5 garlic cloves, minced
- 1 tablespoon lime juice
- ¼ cup butter
- 2 pounds chicken thighs
- 1 teaspoon dried parsley
- 3 green chilies, chopped

Directions

1. Set your Ninja-Foodi to Sauté mode and add onion and garlic
2. Sauté for 3 minutes, add remaining ingredients

3. Lock lid and cook on Medium-HIGH pressure for 20 minutes
4. Release pressure naturally over 10 minutes
5. Serve and enjoy!

Nutrition Values (Per Serving)

- Calories: 282
- Fat: 15g
- Carbohydrates: 6g
- Protein: 27g

Funky-Garlic And turkey Breasts

(Prepping time: 10 minutes\ Cooking time: 17 minutes |For 4 servings)

Ingredients

- ½ teaspoon garlic powder
- 4 tablespoons butter
- ¼ teaspoon dried oregano
- 1 pound turkey breasts, boneless
- 1 teaspoon pepper
- ½ teaspoon salt
- ¼ teaspoon dried basil

Directions

1. Season turkey on both sides generously with garlic, dried oregano, dried basil, salt and pepper
2. Set your Ninja Foodi to sauté mode and add butter, let the butter melt
3. Add turkey breasts and sauté for 2 minutes on each side
4. Lock the lid and select the "Bake/Roast" setting, bake for 15 minutes at 355 degrees F
5. Serve and enjoy once done!

Nutrition Values (Per Serving)

- Calories: 223
- Fat: 13g
- Carbohydrates: 5g
- Protein: 19g

Chapter 5: Savory Beef and Lamb Recipes

Warm And Beefy Meat Loaf

(Prepping time: 10 minutes\ Cooking time: 1 hour 10 minutes |For 6 servings)

Ingredients

- ½ cup onion, chopped
- 2 garlic cloves, minced
- ¼ cup sugar free ketchup
- 1 pound grass fed-lean ground beef
- ½ cup green bell pepper, seeded and chopped
- 1 cup cheddar cheese, grated
- 2 organic eggs, beaten
- 1 teaspoon dried thyme, crushed
- 3 cups fresh spinach, chopped
- 6 cups mozzarella cheese, freshly grated
- Black pepper to taste

Directions

1. Take a bowl and add all of the listed ingredients except cheese and spinach
2. Place a wax paper on a smooth surface and arrange the meat over it
3. Top with spinach, cheese and roll the paper around the paper to form a nice meat loaf
4. Remove wax paper and transfer loaf to your Ninja Foodi
5. Lock lid and select "Bake/Roast" mode, setting the timer to 70 minutes and temperature to 380 degrees F
6. Let it bake and take the dish out once done
7. Serve and enjoy!

Nutrition Values (Per Serving)

- Calories: 409
- Fat: 16g
- Carbohydrates: 5g
- Protein: 56g

Wise Corned Beef

(Prepping time: 10 minutes\ Cooking time: 60 minutes |For 4 servings)

Ingredients

- 4 pounds beef brisket

- 2 garlic cloves, peeled and minced
- 2 yellow onions, peeled and sliced
- 11 ounces celery, thinly sliced
- 1 tablespoon dried dill
- 3 bay leaves
- 4 cinnamon sticks, cut into halves
- Salt and pepper to taste
- 17 ounces water

Directions

1. Take a bowl and add beef, add water and cover, let it soak for 2-3 hours
2. Drain and transfer to the Ninja Foodi
3. Add celery, onions, garlic, bay leaves, dill, cinnamon, dill, salt, pepper and rest of the water to the Ninja Foodi
4. Stir and combine it well
5. Lock lid and cook on HIGH pressure for 50 minutes
6. Release pressure naturally over 10 minutes
7. Transfer meat to cutting board and slice, divide amongst plates and pour the cooking liquid (alongside veggies) over the servings
8. Enjoy!

Nutrition Values (Per Serving)

- Calories: 289
- Fat: 21g
- Carbohydrates: 14g
- Protein: 9g

Elegant Beef Curry

(Prepping time: 10 minutes\ Cooking time: 20 minutes |For 4 servings)

Ingredients

- 2 pounds beef steak, cubed
- 2 tablespoons extra virgin olive oil
- 1 tablespoon Dijon mustard
- 2 and ½ tablespoons curry powder
- 2 yellow onions, peeled and chopped
- 2 garlic cloves, peeled and minced
- 10 ounces canned coconut milk
- 2 tablespoons tomato sauce
- Salt and pepper to taste

Directions

1. Set your Ninja Foodi to "Saute" mode and add oil, let it heat up
2. Add onions, garlic, stir cook for 4 minutes
3. Add mustard, stir and cook for 1 minute
4. Add beef and stir until all sides are browned
5. Add curry powder, salt and pepper, stir cook for 2 minutes
6. Add coconut milk and tomato sauce, stir and cove
7. Lock lid and cook on HIGH pressure for 10 minutes
8. Release pressure naturally over 10 minutes
9. Serve and enjoy!

Nutrition Values (Per Serving)

- Calories: 275
- Fat: 12g
- Carbohydrates: 12g
- Protein: 27g

Mesmerizing Beef Sirloin Steak

(Prepping time: 5 minutes\ Cooking time: 17 minutes |For 4 servings)

Ingredients

- 3 tablespoons butter
- ½ teaspoon garlic powder
- 1-2 pounds beef sirloin steaks
- Salt and pepper to taste
- 1 garlic clove, minced

Directions

1. Set your Ninja Foodi to sauté mode and add butter, let the butter melt
2. Add beef sirloin steaks
3. Saute for 2 minutes on each side
4. Add garlic powder, garlic clove, salt and pepper
5. Lock lid and cook on Medium-HIGH pressure for 15 minutes
6. Release pressure naturally over 10 minutes
7. Transfer prepare Steaks to serving platter, enjoy!

Nutrition Values (Per Serving)

- Calories: 246
- Fat: 13g
- Carbohydrates: 2g
- Protein: 31g

Epic Beef Sausage Soup

(Prepping time: 10 minutes\ Cooking time: 30 minutes |For 6 servings)

Ingredients

- 1 tablespoon extra virgin olive oil
- 6 cups beef broth
- 1 pound organic beef sausage, cooked and sliced
- 2 cups sauerkraut
- 2 celery stalks, chopped
- 1 sweet onion, chopped
- 2 teaspoons garlic, minced
- 2 tablespoons butter
- 1 tablespoon hot mustard
- ½ teaspoon caraway seeds
- ½ cup sour cream
- 2 tablespoons fresh parsley, chopped

Directions

1. Grease the inner pot of your Ninja Foodi with olive oil
2. Add broth, sausage, sauerkraut, celery, onion, garlic, butter, mustard, caraway seeds in the pot
3. Lock lid and cook on HIGH pressure for 30 minutes
4. Quick release pressure
5. Remove lid and stir in sour cream
6. Serve with a topping of parsley
7. Enjoy!

Nutrition Values (Per Serving)

- Calories: 165
- Fat: 4g
- Carbohydrates: 14g
- Protein: 11g

The Indian Beef Delight

(Prepping time: 15 minutes\ Cooking time: 20 minutes |For 4 servings)

Ingredients

- ½ yellow onion, chopped
- 1 tablespoon olive oil

- 2 garlic cloves, minced
- 1 jalapeno pepper, chopped
- 1 cup cherry tomatoes, quartered
- 1 teaspoon fresh lemon juice
- 1-2 pounds grass fed ground beef
- 1-2 pounds fresh collard greens, trimmed and chopped

Spices

- 1 teaspoon cumin, ground
- ½ teaspoon ginger, ground
- 1 teaspoon coriander, ground
- ½ teaspoon fennel seeds, ground
- ½ teaspoon cinnamon, ground
- Salt and pepper to taste
- ½ teaspoon turmeric, ground

Directions

1. Set your Ninja Foodi to sauté mode and add garlic, onions
2. sauté for 3 minutes
3. Add jalapeno pepper, beef and spices
4. Lock lid and cook on Medium-HIGH pressure for 15 minutes
5. Release pressure naturally over 10 minutes, open lid
6. Add tomatoes, collard greens and sauté for 3 minutes
7. Stir in lemon juice, salt and pepper
8. Stir well
9. Once the dish is ready, transfer the dish to your serving bowl and enjoy!

Nutrition Values (Per Serving)

- Calories: 409
- Fat: 16g
- Carbohydrates: 5g
- Protein: 56g

Fresh Korean Braised Ribs

(Prepping time: 10 minutes\ Cooking time: 45 minutes |For 6 servings)

Ingredients

- 1 teaspoon olive oil
- 2 green onions, cut into 1 inch length
- 3 garlic cloves, smashed

- 3 quarter sized ginger slices
- 4 pounds beef short ribs, 3 inches thick, cut into 3 rib portions
- ½ cup water
- ½ cup coconut aminos
- ¼ cup dry white wine
- 2 teaspoons sesame oil
- Mince green onions for serving

Directions

1. Set your Ninja Foodi to "SAUTE" mode and add oil, let it shimmer
2. Add green onions, garlic, ginger, Saute for 1 minute
3. Add short ribs, water, aminos, wine, sesame oil and stir until the ribs are coated well
4. Lock lid and cook on HIGH pressure for 45 minutes
5. Release pressure naturally over 10 minutes
6. Remove short ribs from pot and serve with the cooking liquid
7. Enjoy!

Nutrition Values (Per Serving)

- Calories: 423
- Fat: 35g
- Carbohydrates: 4g
- Protein: 22g

The Classical Corned Beef And Cabbage

(Prepping time: 15 minutes\ Cooking time: 90 minutes |For 4 servings)

Ingredients

- 3 pounds cabbage, cut into eight wedges
- 1 onion, quartered
- 1 celery stalk, quartered
- 1 corned beef spice packet
- 4 cups water
- 1 pound carrots ,peeled and cut to 2 and ½ inch length

Directions

1. Rinse beef thoroughly and add to Ninja Foodi
2. Add onion and celery to the pot
3. Add water and lock lid
4. Cook on HIGH pressure for 90 minutes, quick release pressure
5. Transfer beef to a plate

6. Add carrots, and cabbage to the pot, lock lid again and cook on HIGH pressure for 5 minutes more
7. Quick release pressure
8. Transfer veggies to the plate with corned beef
9. Pass the gravy through a gravy strainer over the beef and serve
10. Enjoy!

Nutrition Values (Per Serving)

- Calories: 531
- Fat: 45g
- Carbohydrates: 9g
- Protein: 25g

Crazy Greek Lamb Gyros

(Prepping time: 10 minutes\ Cooking time: 25 minutes |For 8 servings)

Ingredients

- 8 garlic cloves
- 1 and ½ teaspoon salt
- 2 teaspoons dried oregano
- 1 and ½ cups water
- 2 pounds lamb meat, ground
- 2 teaspoons rosemary
- ½ teaspoon pepper
- 1 small onion, chopped
- 2 teaspoons ground marjoram

Directions

1. Add onions, garlic, marjoram, rosemary, salt and pepper to a food processor
2. Process until combined well, add round lamb meat and process again
3. Press meat mixture gently into a loaf pan
4. Transfer the pan to your Ninja Foodi pot
5. Lock lid and select "Bake/Roast" mode
6. Bake for 25 minutes at 375 degrees F
7. Transfer to serving dish and enjoy!

Nutrition Values (Per Serving)

- Calories: 242
- Fat: 15g
- Carbohydrates: 2.4g
- Protein: 21g

The Ultimate One-Pot Beef Roast

(Prepping time: 10 minutes\ Cooking time: 40 minutes |For 4 servings)

Ingredients

- 2-3 pounds beef, chuck roast
- 4 carrots, chopped
- 3 garlic cloves,
- 2 tablespoons olive oil
- 2 tablespoons Italian seasoning
- 2 stalks celery, chopped
- 1 onion, chopped
- 1 cup beef broth
- 1 cup dry red wine

Directions

1. Set your Ninja Foodi to "Saute" mode and add oil, let it heat up
2. Add roast beef to the pot and cook each side for 1-2 minute until browned
3. Transfer browned beef to plate
4. Add celery, carrot to the pot and top with garlic and onion
5. Add beef broth and wine to the pot, put roast on top of vegies
6. Spread seasoning on top and lock lid, Cook on HIGH pressure for 35 minutes
7. Release pressure naturally over 10 minutes
8. Serve and enjoy!

Nutrition Values (Per Serving)

- Calories: 299
- Fat: 21g
- Carbohydrates: 3g
- Protein: 14g

Easy To Swallow Beef Ribs

(Prepping time: 10 minutes\ Cooking time: 60 minutes |For 6 servings)

Ingredients

- 1 tablespoon sesame oil
- 2 garlic cloves, peeled and smashed
- 1 Knob fresh ginger, peeled and finely chopped
- 1 pinch red pepper flakes
- ¼ cup white wine vinegar
- 2/3 cup coconut aminos

- 2/3 cup beef stock
- 4 pounds beef ribs, chopped in half
- 2 tablespoons arrowroot
- 1-2 tablespoons water

Directions

1. Set your Ninja Foodi to Saute mode and add sesame oil, garlic, ginger, red pepper flakes and Saute for 1 minute
2. Deglaze pot with vinegar and mix in coconut aminos and beef stock
3. Add ribs to the pot and coat them well
4. Lock lid and cook on HIGH pressure for 60 minutes
5. Release pressure naturally over 10 minutes
6. Remove the ribs and keep them on the side
7. Take small bowl and mix in arrowroot and water, stir and mix in the liquid into the pot, set the pot to Saute mode and cook until the liquid reaches your desired consistency
8. Put the ribs under a broiler to brown them slightly (also possible to do this in the Ninja Foodi using the Air Crisping lid)
9. Serve ribs with the cooking liquid
10. Enjoy!

Nutrition Values (Per Serving)

- Calories: 307
- Fat: 10g
- Carbohydrates: 5g
- Protein: 32g

Everyday Lamb Roast

(Prepping time: 10 minutes\ Cooking time: 60 minutes |For 6 servings)

Ingredients

- 2 pounds lamb roasted wegmans
- 1 cup onion soup
- 1 cup beef broth
- Salt and pepper to taste

Directions

1. Transfer lamb roast to your Ninja Foodi pot
2. Add onion soup, beef broth, salt and pepper
3. Lock lid and cook on Medium-HIGH pressure for 55 minutes
4. Release pressure naturally over 10 minutes
5. Transfer to serving bowl, serve and enjoy!

Nutrition Values (Per Serving)

- Calories: 349
- Fat: 18g
- Carbohydrates: 2.9g
- Protein: 39g

The Gentle Beef And Broccoli Dish

(Prepping time: 10 minutes\ Cooking time: 20 minutes |For 4 servings)

Ingredients

- 3 pounds beef chuck roast, cut into thin strips
- 1 tablespoon olive oil
- 1 yellow onion, peeled and chopped
- ½ cup beef stock
- 1 pound broccoli florets
- 2 teaspoons toasted sesame oil
- 2 tablespoons arrowroot

For Marinade

- 1 cup coconut aminos
- 1 tablespoon sesame oil
- 2 tablespoons fish sauce
- 5 garlic cloves, peeled and minced
- 3 red peppers, dried and crushed
- ½ teaspoon Chinese five spice powder
- Toasted sesame seeds, for serving

Directions

1. Take a bowl and mix in coconut aminos, fish sauce, 1 tablespoon sesame oil, garlic, five spice powder, crushed red pepper and stir
2. Add beef strips to the bowl and toss to coat
3. Keep it on the side for 10 minutes
4. Set your Ninja Foodi to "Saute" mode and add oil, let it heat up, add onion and stir cook for 4 minutes
5. Add beef and marinade, stir cook for 2 minutes. Add stock and stir
6. Lock the pressure lid of Ninja Foodi and cook on HIGH pressure for 5 minutes
7. Release pressure naturally over 10 minutes
8. Mix arrowroot with ¼ cup liquid from the pot and gently pour the mixture back to the pot and stir

9. Place a steamer basket in the pot and add broccoli to the steamer rack, lock lid and cook on HIGH pressure for 3 minutes more, quick release pressure
10. Divide the dish between plates and serve with broccoli, toasted sesame seeds and enjoy!

Nutrition Values (Per Serving)

- Calories: 433
- Fat: 27g
- Carbohydrates: 8g
- Protein: 20g

The Juicy Beef Chili

(Prepping time: 10 minutes\ Cooking time: 40 minutes |For 4 servings)

Ingredients

- 1 and ½ pounds ground beef
- 1 sweet onion, peeled and chopped
- Salt and pepper to taste
- 28 ounces canned tomatoes, diced
- 17 ounces beef stock
- 6 garlic clove, peeled and chopped
- 7 jalapeno peppers, diced
- 2 tablespoons olive oil
- 4 carrots, peeled and chopped
- 3 tablespoons chili powder
- 1 bay leaf
- 1 teaspoon chili powder

Directions

1. Set your Ninja Foodi to "Saute" mode and add half of oil, let it heat up
2. Add beef and stir brown for 8 minutes, transfer to a bowl
3. Add remaining oil to the pot and let it heat up, add carrots, onion, jalapenos, garlic and stir Saute for 4 minutes
4. Add tomatoes and stir
5. Add bay leaf, stock, chili powder, chili powder, salt, pepper and beef, stir and lock lid
6. Cook on HIGH pressure for 25 minutes
7. Release pressure naturally over 10 minutes
8. Stir the chili and serve
9. Enjoy!

Nutrition Values (Per Serving)

- Calories: 448

- Fat: 22g
- Carbohydrates: 7g
- Protein: 15g

Generous Ground Beef Stew

(Prepping time: 5 minutes\ Cooking time: 5 minutes |For 4 servings)

Ingredients

- 1 tablespoon olive oil
- 1 and ½ pounds lean ground beef
- 1 large yellow onion, chopped
- 1 teaspoon ground cinnamon
- 1 teaspoon ground cumin
- ½ teaspoon dried sage
- ½ teaspoon dried oregano
- ½ teaspoon salt
- ½ teaspoon pepper
- 2 tablespoons almond meal
- 2 and ½ cups beef broth
- 2 teaspoons stevia

Directions

1. Set your Ninja Foodi to Saute mode and add oil, let it heat up
2. Add ground beef and stir for about 5 minutes until browned
3. Add onion, and cook for 3 minutes more
4. Stir in cinnamon, cumin, sage, oregano, salt, pepper and cook for 1 minute
5. Stir in almond meal and cook for 1 minute more
6. Stir in broth
7. Lock lid and cook on HIGH pressure for 5 minutes, release pressure naturally over 10 minutes
8. Stir well until loosely covered, serve and enjoy!

Nutrition Values (Per Serving)

- Calories: 480
- Fat: 23g
- Carbohydrates: 12g
- Protein: 20g

Chapter 6: Great Pork Recipes

Mesmerizing Pork Carnitas

(Prepping time: 10 minutes\ Cooking time: 25 minutes |For 4 servings)

Ingredients

- 2 pounds pork butt, chopped into 2 inch pieces
- 1 teaspoon salt
- ½ teaspoon oregano
- ½ teaspoon cumin
- 1 yellow onion, cut into half
- 6 garlic cloves, peeled and crushed
- ½ cup chicken broth

Directions

1. Insert a pan into your Ninja Foodi and add pork
2. Season with salt, cumin, oregano and mix well, making sure that the pork is well seasoned
3. Take the orange and squeeze the orange juice all over
4. Add squeezed orange to into the insert pan as well
5. Add garlic cloves and onions
6. Pour ½ cup chicken broth into the pan
7. Lock the lid of the Ninja Foodi, making sure that the valve is sealed well
8. Set pressure to HIGH and let it cook for 20 minutes
9. Once the timer beeps, quick release the pressure
10. Open the lid and take out orange, garlic cloves, and onions
11. Set your Nina Foodi to Sauté mode and adjust the temperature to medium-high
12. Let the liquid simmer for 10-15 minutes
13. After most of the liquid has been reduced, press stop button
14. Close the Ninja Foodi with "Air Crisp" lid
15. Pressure broil option and set timer to 8 minutes
16. Take the meat and put it in wraps
17. Garnish with cilantro and enjoy!

Nutrition Values (Per Serving)
- Calories: 355
- Fat: 13g
- Carbohydrates: 9g
- Protein: 43g

Mustard Dredged Pork Chops

(Prepping time: 10 minutes\ Cooking time: 30 minutes |For 4 servings)

Ingredients

- 2 tablespoons butter
- 2 tablespoons Dijon mustard (Keto-Friendly)
- 4 pork chops
- Salt and pepper to taste
- 1 tablespoon fresh rosemary, coarsely chopped

Directions

1. Take a bowl and add pork chops, cover with Dijon mustard and carefully sprinkle rosemary, salt and pepper
2. Let it marinate for 2 hours
3. Add butter and marinated pork chops to your Ninja Foodi pot
4. Lock lid and cook on Low-Medium Pressure for 30 minutes
5. Release pressure naturally over 10 minutes
6. Take the dish out, serve and enjoy!

Nutrition Values (Per Serving)

- Calories: 315
- Fat: 26g
- Carbohydrates: 1g
- Protein: 18g

Authentic Beginner Friendly Pork Belly

(Prepping time: 10 minutes\ Cooking time: 40 minutes |For 4 servings)

Ingredients

- 1 pound pork belly
- ½-1 cup white wine vinegar
- 1 garlic clove
- 1 tablespoon olive oil
- Salt and pepper to taste

Directions

1. Set your Ninja Foodi to "SAUTE" mode and add oil, let it heat up
2. Add pork and sear for 2-3 minutes until both sides are golden and crispy
3. Add vinegar until about a quarter inch, season with salt, pepper and garlic
4. Add garlic clove and Saute until the liquid comes to a boil

5. Lock lid and cook on HIGH pressure for 40 minutes

6. Once done, quick release pressure

7. Slice the meat and serve with the sauce

8. Enjoy!

Nutrition Values (Per Serving)

- Calories: 331
- Fat: 21g
- Carbohydrates: 2g
- Protein: 19g

Deliciously Spicy Pork Salad Bowl

(Prepping time: 10 minutes\ Cooking time: 90 minutes |For 6 servings)

Ingredients

- 4 pounds pork shoulder
- Butter as needed
- 2 teaspoons salt
- 2 cups chicken stock
- 1 teaspoon smoked paprika powder
- 1 teaspoon garlic powder
- 1 teaspoon black pepper
- 1 pinch dried oregano leaves
- 4 tablespoons coconut oil
- 6 garlic cloves

Directions

1. Remove rind from pork and cut meat from bone, slice into large chunks

2. Trim fat off met

3. Set your Foodi to Saute mode and add oil, let it heat up

4. Once the oil is hot, layer chunks of meat in the bottom of the pot and Saute for around 30 minutes until browned

5. While the meat are being browned, peel garlic cloves and cut into small chunks

6. Once the meat is browned, transfer it to a large sized bowl

7. Add a few tablespoons of chicken stock to the pot an deglaze it, scraping off browned bits

8. Transfer browned bits to the bowl with meat chunks

9. Repeat if any more meat are left

10. Once done, add garlic, oregano leaves, smoked paprika,. Garlic powder, pepper and salt to the meat owl and mix it up

11. Add all chicken stock to pot and bring to a simmer over Saute mode

12. Once done, return seasoned meat to the pot and lock lid, cook on HIGH pressure for 45 minutes. Release pressure naturally over 10 minutes

13. Open lid and shred the meat using fork, transfer shredded meat to a bowl and pour cooking liquid through a mesh to separate fat into the bowl with shredded meat

14. Serve with lime and enjoy!

Nutrition Values (Per Serving)

- Calories: 307
- Fat: 23g
- Carbohydrates: 8g
- Protein: 15g

Special "Swiss" Pork chops

(Prepping time: 5 minutes\ Cooking time: 18 minutes |For 4 servings)

Ingredients

- ½ cup Swiss cheese, shredded
- 4 pork chops, bone-in
- 6 bacon strips, cut in half
- Salt and pepper to taste
- 1 tablespoon butter

Directions

1. Season pork chops with salt and pepper

2. Set your Foodi to sauté mode and add butter, let the butter heat up

3. Add pork chops and sauté for 3 minutes on each side

4. Add bacon strips and Swiss cheese

5. Lock lid and cook on Medium-LOW pressure for 15 minutes

6. Release pressure naturally over 10 minutes

7. Transfer steaks to serving platter, serve and enjoy!

Nutrition Values (Per Serving)

- Calories: 483
- Fat: 40g
- Carbohydrates: 0.7g
- Protein: 27g

Perfect Sichuan Pork Soup

(Prepping time: 10 minutes\ Cooking time: 20 minutes |For 6 servings)

Ingredients

- 2 tablespoons olive oil
- 1 tablespoon garlic, minced
- 1 tablespoon fresh ginger, minced
- 2 tablespoons coconut aminos
- 2 tablespoons black vinegar
- 1-2 teaspoons stevia
- 1-2 teaspoons salt
- ½ onion, sliced
- 1 pound pork shoulder, cut into 2 inch chunks
- 2 pepper corns, crushed
- 3 cups water
- 3-4 cups bok choy, chopped
- ¼ cup fresh cilantro, chopped

Directions

1. Pre-heat your Ninja Foodi by setting it to Saute mode on HIGH settings
2. Once the inner pot it hot enough, add oil and let heat until shimmering
3. Add garlic and ginger and Saute for 1-2 minutes
4. Add coconut aminos, vinegar, sweetener, pepper corn, salt, onion, pork, water and stir
5. Lock lid and cook on HIGH pressure for 20 minutes
6. Release pressure naturally over 10 minutes
7. Open lid and add bok choy, close lid and let it cook in the remaining heat for 10 minutes
8. Ladle soup into serving bowl and serve with topping of cilantro
9. Enjoy!

Nutrition Values (Per Serving)

- Calories: 256
- Fat: 20g
- Carbohydrates: 5g
- Protein: 14g

Healthy Cranberry Keto-Friendly BBQ Pork

(Prepping time: 10 minutes\ Cooking time: 45 minutes |For 4 servings)

Ingredients

- 3-4 pounds pork shoulder, boneless, fat trimmed

For Sauce

- 3 tablespoons liquid smoke
- 2 tablespoons tomato paste
- 2 cups fresh cranberries
- ¼ cup hot sauce (Keto-Friendly)
- 1/3 cup blackstrap molasses
- ½ cup water
- ½ cup apple cider vinegar
- 1 teaspoon salt
- 1 tablespoons adobo sauce (Keto Friendly and Sugar Free)
- 1 cup tomato puree (Keto-Friendly and Sugar Free)
- 1 chipotle pepper in adobo sauce, diced

Directions

1. Cut pork against halves/thirds and keep it on the side
2. Set your Ninja Foodi to "SAUTE" mode and let it heat up
3. Add cranberries and water to the pot
4. Let them simmer for 4-5 minutes until cranberries start to pop, add rest of the sauce ingredients and simmer for 5 minutes more
5. Add pork to the pot and lock lid
6. Cook on HIGH pressure for 40 minutes
7. Quick release pressure
8. Use fork to shred the pork and serve on your favorite greens

Nutrition Values (Per Serving)

- Calories: 250
- Fat: 17g
- Carbohydrates: 5g
- Protein: 15g

Decisive Kalua Pork

(Prepping time: 10 minutes\ Cooking time: 90 minutes |For 4 servings)

Ingredients

- 4 pounds pork shoulder, cut into half
- ½ cup water
- 2 tablespoons olive oil
- Salt and pepper to taste
- 1 tablespoon liquid smoke
- Steamer green beans for serving (optional)

Directions

1. Set your Ninja Foodi to "SAUTE" mode and add oil, let it heat up
2. Add pork, salt and pepper, brown each side for 3 minutes until both sides are slightly browned
3. Transfer them to a plate
4. Add water, liquid smoke to the pot and return the meat, stir
5. Lock lid and cook on HIGH pressure for 90 minutes, release pressure naturally over 10 minutes
6. Transfer meat to cutting board and shred using 2 forks, divide between serving plates and serve with the cooking liquid on top, add green beans on the side if you prefer
7. Enjoy!

Nutrition Values (Per Serving)

- Calories: 357
- Fat: 28g
- Carbohydrates: 2g
- Protein: 20g

Easy-Going Kid Friendly Pork Chops

(Prepping time: 15 minutes\ Cooking time: 5-10 minutes |For 4 servings)

Ingredients

- 3-4 pork chops -12 to ¾ inch thick each
- 1 egg, beaten
- 1-2 cups Almond flour as needed
- Salt and pepper to taste
- 1-2 cups almond meal
- ½ cup onions, chopped
- 2-4 garlic cloves, squashed and chopped
- 1 tablespoons butter
- 1-2 tablespoons coconut oil

Directions

1. Set your Ninja Foodi to "Saute" mode and add butter, let it heat up
2. Dredge the pork chops in beaten egg, then in flour and finally in almond meal
3. Add them to the pot and brown all sides
4. Add onions and cook for a minute
5. Add garlic and cook for 1 minute more
6. Transfer the browned meat, onion and garlic to a plate, make sure to keep the drippings in the pot
7. Add 2-3 tablespoons of water and place and place a steamer rack in your pot
8. Add browned pork chops on the steamer and lock lid

9. Cook on HIGH Pressure for 5 minutes, once done, let the pressure release naturally over 10 minutes

10. Remove from pot and serve

11. Enjoy!

Nutrition Values (Per Serving)

- Calories: 446
- Fat: 25g
- Carbohydrates: 6g
- Protein: 21g

Amazing Mexican Pulled Pork Lettuce

(Prepping time: 10 minutes\ Cooking time: 60 minutes |For 4 servings)

Ingredients

- 4 pounds pork roast
- 1 head butter lettuce, washed and dried
- 2 carrots, grated
- 2 tablespoons olive oil
- 2 lime wedges
- 1 onion, chopped
- 1 tablespoon salt
- 2-3 cups water

For Spice Mix

- 1 tablespoons unsweetened cocoa powder
- 2 teaspoons oregano
- 1 teaspoon red pepper flakes
- 1 teaspoon garlic powder
- 1 teaspoon white pepper
- 1 teaspoon cumin
- 1/8 teaspoon cayenne
- 1/8 teaspoon coriander

Directions

1. Marinate pork overnight by transferring the meat to a bowl and mixing in all of the spices

2. Set your Ninja Foodi to "SAUTE" mode and add roast, let it brown

3. Add 2-3 cups water to fully submerge the roast

4. Lock lid and cook on HIGH pressure for 55 minutes

5. Release pressure naturally over 10 minutes

6. Set your pot to "SAUTE" mode again and take out the meat, shred the meat and keep it on the side

7. Reduce the liquid by half and strain/skim any excess fat

8. Mix pork with cooking liquid and serve with lettuce, grated carrots, squire of lime and any other topping you desire

9. Enjoy!

Nutrition Values (Per Serving)

- Calories: 245
- Fat: 18g
- Carbohydrates: 4g
- Protein: 13g

Chapter 7: Graceful Seafood And Fish Recipes

Small-Time Herby Cods

(Prepping time: 5 minutes\ Cooking time: 8 minutes |For 4 servings)

Ingredients

- 4 garlic cloves, minced
- 2 teaspoons coconut aminos
- ¼ cup butter
- 6 whole eggs
- 2 small onions, chopped
- 3 (4 ounces each) skinless cod fish fillets, cut into rectangular pieces
- 2 green chilies, chopped
- Salt and pepper to taste

Directions

1. Take a shallow dish and add all ingredients except cod, beat the mixture well
2. Dip each fillet into the mixture and keep it on the side
3. Transfer prepared fillets to your Ninja Foodi Crisping basket and transfer basket to Pot
4. Lock Crisping lid and cook on "Air Crisp" mode for 8 minutes at 330 degrees F
5. Serve and enjoy!

Nutrition Values (Per Serving)

- Calories: 409
- Fat: 25g
- Carbohydrates: 7g
- Protein: 37g

Hearty Swordfish Meal

(Prepping time: 5 minutes\ Cooking time: 150 minutes |For 4 servings)

Ingredients

- 5 swordfish fillets
- ½ a cup of melted clarified butter
- 6 garlic cloves, chopped
- 1 tablespoon black pepper

Directions

1. Take a mixing bowl and add garlic, clarified butter, black pepper
2. Take a parchment paper and add the fillet
3. Cover and wrap the fish
4. Keep repeating until the fillets are wrapped up
5. Transfer wrapped fish to Ninja Foodi pot and lock lid
6. Allow them to cook for 2 and a ½ hour at high pressure
7. Release the pressure naturally
8. Serve and enjoy!

Nutrition Values (Per Serving)

- Calories: 379
- Fat: 26g
- Carbohydrates: 1g
- Protein: 34g

Gentle And Simple Fish Stew

(Prepping time: 5 minutes\ Cooking time: 20 minutes |For 4 servings)

Ingredients

- 3 cups fish stock
- 1 onion, diced
- 1 cup broccoli, chopped
- 2 cups celery stalks, chopped
- 1 and ½ cups cauliflower, diced
- 1 carrot, sliced
- 1 pound white fish fillets, chopped
- 1 cup heavy cream
- 1 bay leaf
- 2 tablespoons butter
- ¼ teaspoon pepper
- ½ teaspoon salt
- ¼ teaspoon garlic powder

Directions

1. Set your Ninja Foodi to Saute mode and add butter, let it melt
2. Add onion and carrots, cook for 3 minutes
3. Stir in remaining ingredients
4. Lock lid and cook on HIGH pressure for 4 minutes
5. Naturally, release pressure over 10 minutes

6. Discard bay leaf

7. Serve and enjoy!

Nutrition Values (Per Serving)

- Calories: 298
- Fat: 18g
- Carbohydrates: 6g
- Protein: 24g

Cool Shrimp Zoodles

(Prepping time: 5 minutes\ Cooking time: 3 minutes |For 4 servings)

Ingredients

- 4 cups zoodles
- 1 tablespoon basil, chopped
- 2 tablespoons Ghee
- 1 cup vegetable stock
- 2 garlic cloves, minced
- 2 tablespoons olive oil
- ½ lemon
- ½ teaspoon paprika

Directions

1. Set your Ninja Foodi to Saute mode and add ghee, let it heat up

2. Add olive oil as well

3. Add garlic and cook for 1 minute

4. Add lemon juice, shrimp and cook for 1 minute

5. Stir in rest of the ingredients and lock lid, cook on LOW pressure for 5 minutes

6. Quick release pressure and serve

7. Enjoy!

Nutrition Values (Per Serving)

- Calories: 277
- Fat: 6g
- Carbohydrates: 5g
- Protein: 27g

Heartfelt Sesame Fish

(Prepping time: 8 minutes\ Cooking time: 8 minutes |For 4 servings)

Ingredients

- 1 and ½ pound salmon fillet
- 1 teaspoon sesame seeds
- 1 teaspoon butter, melted
- ½ teaspoon salt
- 1 tablespoon apple cider vinegar
- ¼ teaspoon rosemary, dried

Directions

1. Take apple cider vinegar and spray it to the salmon fillets
2. Then add dried rosemary, sesame seeds, butter and salt
3. Mix them well
4. Take butter sauce and brush the salmon properly
5. Place the salmon on the rack and lower the air fryer lid
6. Set the air fryer mode
7. Cook the fish for 8 minutes at 360 F
8. Serve hot and enjoy!

Nutrition Values (Per Serving)

- Calories: 239
- Fat: 11.2g
- Carbohydrates: 0.3g
- Protein: 33.1g

Awesome Sock-Eye Salmon

(Prepping time: 5 minutes\ Cooking time: 5 minutes |For 4 servings)

Ingredients

- 4 sockeye salmon fillets
- 1 teaspoon Dijon mustard
- ¼ teaspoon garlic, minced
- ¼ teaspoon onion powder
- ¼ teaspoon lemon pepper
- ½ teaspoon garlic powder
- ¼ teaspoon salt
- 2 tablespoons olive oil

- 1 and ½ cup of water

Directions

1. Take a bowl and add mustard, lemon juice, onion powder, lemon pepper, garlic powder, salt, olive oil
2. Brush spice mix over salmon
3. Add water to Instant Pot
4. Place rack and place salmon fillets on rack
5. Lock lid and cook on LOW pressure for 7 minutes
6. Quick release pressure
7. Serve and enjoy!

Nutrition Values (Per Serving)

- Calories: 353
- Fat: 25g
- Carbohydrates: 0.6g
- Protein: 40g

Buttered Up Scallops

(Prepping time: 10 minutes\ Cooking time: 5 minutes |For 4 servings)

Ingredients

- 4 garlic cloves, minced
- 4 tablespoons rosemary, chopped
- 2 pounds sea scallops
- 12 cup butter
- Salt and pepper to taste

Directions

1. Set your Ninja Foodi to Saute mode and add butter, rosemary, and garlic
2. Saute for 1 minute
3. Add scallops, salt, and pepper
4. Saute for 2 minutes
5. Lock Crisping lid and Crisp for 3 minutes at 350 degrees F
6. Serve and enjoy!

Nutrition Values (Per Serving)

- Calories: 279
- Fat: 16g

- Carbohydrates: 5g
- Protein: 25g

Awesome Cherry Tomato Mackerel
(Prepping time: 5 minutes\ Cooking time: 7 minutes |For 4 servings)

Ingredients

- 4 Mackerel fillets
- ¼ teaspoon onion powder
- ¼ teaspoon lemon powder
- ¼ teaspoon garlic powder
- ½ teaspoon salt
- 2 cups cherry tomatoes
- 3 tablespoons melted butter
- 1 and ½ cups of water
- 1 tablespoon black olives

Directions

1. Grease baking dish and arrange cherry tomatoes at the bottom of the dish
2. Top with fillets sprinkle all spices
3. Drizzle melted butter over
4. Add water to your Ninja Foodi
5. Lower rack in Ninja Foodi and place baking dish on top of the rack
6. Lock lid and cook on LOW pressure for 7 minutes
7. Quick release pressure
8. Serve and enjoy!

Nutrition Values (Per Serving)

- Calories: 325
- Fat: 24g
- Carbohydrates: 2g
- Protein: 21g

Lovely Air Fried Scallops
(Prepping time: 5 minutes\ Cooking time: 5 minutes |For 4 servings)

Ingredients

- 12 scallops

- 3 tablespoons olive oil
- Salt and pepper to taste

Directions

1. Gently rub scallops with salt, pepper, and oil
2. Transfer to your Ninja Foodie's insert, and place the insert in your Foodi
3. Lock Air Crisping lid and cook for 4 minutes at 390 degrees F
4. Half through, make sure to give them a nice flip and keep cooking
5. Serve warm and enjoy!

Nutrition Values (Per Serving)

- Calories: 372
- Fat: 11g
- Carbohydrates: 0.9g
- Protein: 63g

Packets Of Lemon And Dill Cod

(Prepping time: 10 minutes\ Cooking time: 5-10 minutes |For 4 servings)

Ingredients

- 2 tilapia cod fillets
- Salt, pepper and garlic powder to taste
- 2 sprigs fresh dill
- 4 slices lemon
- 2 tablespoons butter

Directions

1. Layout 2 large squares of parchment paper
2. Place fillet in center of each parchment square and season with salt, pepper and garlic powder
3. On each fillet, place 1 sprig of dill, 2 lemon slices, 1 tablespoon butter
4. Place trivet at the bottom of your Ninja Foodi
5. Add 1 cup water into the pot
6. Close parchment paper around fillets and fold to make a nice seal
7. Place both packets in your pot
8. Lock lid and cook on HIGH pressure for 5 minutes
9. Quick release pressure
10. Serve and enjoy!

Nutrition Values (Per Serving)

- Calories: 259

- Fat: 11g
- Carbohydrates: 8g
- Protein: 20g

Adventurous Sweet And Sour Fish

(Prepping time: 10 minutes\ Cooking time: 6 minutes |For 4 servings)

Ingredients

- 2 drops liquid stevia
- ¼ cup butter
- 1 pound fish chunks
- 1 tablespoon vinegar
- Salt and pepper to taste

Directions

1. Set your Ninja Foodi to Saute mode and add butter, let it melt
2. Add fish chunks and Saute for 3 minutes
3. Add stevia, salt, and pepper, stir
4. Lock Crisping Lid and cook on "Air Crisp" mode for 3 minutes at 360 degrees F
5. Serve once done and enjoy!

Nutrition Values (Per Serving)

- Calories: 274
- Fat: 15g
- Carbohydrates: 2g
- Protein: 33g

Garlic And Lemon Prawn Delight

(Prepping time: 5 minutes\ Cooking time: 5 minutes |For 4 servings)

Ingredients

- 2 tablespoons olive oil
- 1 pound prawns
- 2 tablespoons garlic, minced
- 2/3 cup fish stock
- 1 tablespoon butter

- 2 tablespoons lemon juice
- 1 tablespoon lemon zest
- Salt and pepper to taste

Directions

1. Set your Ninja Foodi to Saute mode and add butter and oil, let it heat up
2. Stir in remaining ingredients
3. Lock lid and cook on LOW pressure for 5 minutes
4. Quick release pressure
5. Serve and enjoy!

Nutrition Values (Per Serving)

- Calories: 236
- Fat: 12g
- Carbohydrates: 2g
- Protein: 27g

Lovely Carb Soup

(Prepping time: 5 minutes\ Cooking time: 6-7 hours |For 4 servings)

Ingredients

- 1 cup crab meat, cubed
- 1 tablespoon garlic, minced
- Salt as needed
- Red chili flakes as needed
- 3 cups vegetable broth
- 1 teaspoon salt

Directions

1. Coat the crab cubes in lime juice and let them sit for a while
2. Add the all ingredients (including marinated crab meat) to your Ninja Foodi and lock lid
3. Cook on SLOW COOK MODE (MEDIUM) for 3 hours
4. Let it sit for a while
5. Unlock lid and set to Saute mode, simmer the soup for 5 minutes more on LOW
6. Stir and check to season
7. Enjoy!

Nutrition Values (Per Serving)

- Calories: 201
- Fat: 11g
- Carbohydrates: 12g
- Protein: 13g

The Rich Guy Lobster And Butter

(Prepping time: 15 minutes\ Cooking time: 20 minutes |For 4 servings)

Ingredients

- 6 Lobster Tails
- 4 garlic cloves,
- ¼ cup butter

Directions

1. Preheat the Ninja Foodi to 400 degrees F at first
2. Open the lobster tails gently by using kitchen scissors
3. Remove the lobster meat gently from the shells but keep it inside the shells
4. Take a plate and place it
5. Add some butter in a pan and allow it melt
6. Put some garlic cloves in it and heat it over medium-low heat
7. Pour the garlic butter mixture all over the lobster tail meat
8. Let the fryer to broil the lobster at 130 degrees F
9. Remove the lobster meat from Ninja Foodi and set aside
10. Use a fork to pull out the lobster meat from the shells entirely
11. Pour some garlic butter over it if needed
12. Serve and enjoy!

Nutrition Values (Per Serving)

- Calories: 160
- Fat: 1g
- Carbohydrates: 1g
- Protein: 20g

Tomato And Shrimp Medley

(Prepping time: 10 minutes\ Cooking time: 5 minutes |For 4 servings)

Ingredients

- 3 tablespoons unsalted butter
- 1 tablespoon garlic
- ½ teaspoon red pepper flakes
- 1 and ½ cup onion, chopped
- 1 can (14 and ½ ounces) tomatoes, diced
- 1 teaspoon dried oregano
- 1 teaspoon salt
- 1 pound frozen shrimp, peeled
- 1 cup crumbled feta cheese
- ½ cup black olives, sliced
- ½ cup parsley, chopped

Directions

1. Pre-heat your Ninja Foodi by setting in in the Saute mode on HIGH settings, add butter and let it melt
2. Add garlic, pepper flakes, cook for 1 minute
3. Add onion, tomato, oregano, salt and stir well
4. Add frozen shrimp
5. Lock lid and cook on HIGH pressure for 1 minute
6. Quick release pressure
7. Mix shrimp with tomato broth, let it cool and serve with a sprinkle of feta, olives and parsley
8. Enjoy!

Nutrition Values (Per Serving)

- Calories: 361
- Fat: 22g
- Carbohydrates: 11g
- Protein: 30g

The Smoked White Fish

(Prepping time: 10 minutes\ Cooking time: 2 hours |For 4 servings)

Ingredients

- 2 pounds Whitefish fillets, raw
- 1 tablespoon onion powder
- ½ teaspoon cumin
- 1 tablespoon paprika
- 1 tablespoon garlic powder

- 1 tablespoon olive oil
- Fresh lemon juice
- Fresh cilantro, chopped
- Salt and pepper to taste

Directions

1. Set up your Ninja Foodi to 200 degrees F on a low heat setting
2. Use olive oil to brush the fish fillets
3. Add cumin, garlic powder, onion powder, paprika, salt, and pepper in a bowl and mix them well
4. Rub this prepared seasoning all over the pork from all the sides
5. Spray some olive oil more on the fillets
6. Put the seasoned fillets on the rack and put it inside the Ninja Foodi at a low temperature
7. Cook for 2 hours
8. Garnish it with chopped cilantro and fresh lemon juice
9. Serve and enjoy!

Nutrition Values (Per Serving)

- Calories: 142
- Fat: 2g
- Carbohydrates: 0g
- Protein: 30g

Cool Lemon And Dill Fish Packages

(Prepping time: 10 minutes\ Cooking time: 5-10 minutes |For 4 servings)

Ingredients

- 2 tilapia cod fillets
- Salt, pepper and garlic powder to taste
- 2 sprigs fresh dill
- 4 slices lemon
- 2 tablespoons butter

Directions

11. Lay out 2 large squares of parchment paper
12. Place fillet in center of each parchment square and season with salt, pepper and garlic powder
13. On each fillet, place 1 sprig of dill, 2 lemon slices, 1 tablespoon butter
14. Place trivet at the bottom of your Ninja Foodi
15. Add 1 cup water into the pot
16. Close parchment paper around fillets and fold to make a nice seal

17. Place both packets in your pot
18. Lock lid and cook on HIGH pressure for 5 minutes
19. Quick release pressure
20. Serve and enjoy!

Nutrition Values (Per Serving)

- Calories: 259
- Fat: 11g
- Carbohydrates: 8g
- Protein: 20g

Heart-Throb Buttery Scallops

(Prepping time: 10 minutes\ Cooking time: 15 minutes |For 4 servings)

Ingredients

- 4 garlic cloves, minced
- 4 tablespoons fresh rosemary, chopped
- 2 pounds sea scallops
- ½ cup butter
- Salt and pepper to taste

Directions

1. Set your Ninja Foodi to Saute mode and add butter and let it melt
2. Add rosemary, garlic and Saute for 1 minute
3. Add sea scallops, salt and pepper
4. Saute for 2 minutes more
5. Lock Crisping Lid and cook on "Air Crisp" mode for 3 minutes at 350 degrees F
6. Once done, serve and enjoy!

Nutrition Values (Per Serving)

- Calories: 279
- Fat: 16g
- Carbohydrates: 4g
- Protein: 25g

Sensational Coconut Fish Curry

(Prepping time: 10 minutes\ Cooking time: 5-10 minutes |For 4 servings)

Ingredients

- 1 and ½ pounds white fish fillets, rinsed and cut into bite sized pieces
- 1 heaping cup cherry tomatoes
- 2 green chilies, sliced into strips
- 2 garlic cloves, finely chopped
- 1 tablespoon ginger, freshly grated
- 6 curry leaves such as bay leaves
- 1 tablespoon ground coriander
- 1 tablespoon ground cumin
- ½ teaspoon ground turmeric
- 1 teaspoon chili powder
- ½ teaspoon ground fenugreek
- 2 cups coconut milk, unsweetened
- 1 teaspoon olive oil
- Salt to taste
- Lemon juice to taste

Directions

1. Set your Ninja Foodi to Saute mode and add oil and curry leaves
2. Gently fry for 1 minute, add onion, garlic, ginger and Saute until onion are tender
3. Add coriander, turmeric, chili powder, fenugreek (all ground) and Saute with onions for 1 minute
4. Deglaze pot with coconut milk, scraping browned bits
5. Add green chilies, tomatoes and fish and stir to coat
6. Lock lid and cook on HIGH pressure for 3 minutes, quick release pressure
7. Open lid and season with salt and lemon juice
8. Enjoy!

Nutrition Values (Per Serving)

- Calories: 276
- Fat: 21g
- Carbohydrates: 4g
- Protein: 18g

Warm Cajun Bass Stew

(Prepping time: 10 minutes\ Cooking time: 28 minutes |For 6 servings)

Ingredients

- 1 pound sea bass fillets, patted dry and cut into 2 inch chunks
- 3 tablespoons Cajun seasoning, divided
- ½ teaspoon salt
- 2 tablespoons extra virgin olive oil

- 2 yellow onion, diced
- 2 bell peppers, diced
- 4 celery stalks, diced
- 1 can (28 ounces) diced tomatoes, drained
- ¼ cup tomato paste
- 1 and ½ cups veggie broth
- 2 pounds large shrimp, peeled and deveined

Directions

1. Set your Pot to Saute mode at a temperature of Medium-HIGH heat, let it pre-heat for 5 minutes
2. Season sea bass on both sides with 1 and ½ tablespoons Cajun seasoning and ¼ teaspoon salt
3. Put 1 tablespoon oil and sea bass in your pre-heated pot
4. Saute for 4 minutes
5. Add remaining 1 tablespoon oil and onions to the pot and cook for 3 minutes, add bell peppers, celery, and 1 and ½ tablespoons Cajun seasoning to the pot
6. Cook for 2 minutes more
7. Add sea bass, diced tomatoes, tomato paste, broth to the pot, place the lid and seal the valves
8. Cook on HIGH pressure for 5 minutes, quick release the pressure once did
9. Set your pot to Saute mode again with the temperature set at Medium-HIGH mode and add shrimp
10. Place lid and seal the pressure valve, cook for 4 minutes until the shrimp is opaque
11. Season with ¼ teaspoon salt and serve, enjoy!

Nutrition Values (Per Serving)

- Calories: 326
- Fat: 9g
- Carbohydrates: 10g
- Protein: 46g

The Great Lobster Bisque

(Prepping time: 10 minutes\ Cooking time: 10 minutes |For 4 servings)

Ingredients

- 2 teaspoons unsalted butter
- 1 onion, chopped
- 1 tablespoon garlic, minced
- 1 tablespoon fresh ginger, minced
- 2 cups vegetable broth
- 1 cup tomatoes, chopped
- 3 cups cauliflower, chopped
- 2 tablespoons Keto-Friendly pesto

- ½ teaspoon salt
- 1 -2 teaspoons fresh ground black pepper
- 1 pound cooked lobster meat
- 1 cup heavy whip cream

Directions

1. Pre-heat your Ninja Foodi by setting to Saute mode on HIGH settings
2. Once the inner pot is hot, add butter and let it heat up
3. Once the butter is shimmering, add onion, garlic and ginger
4. Saute for 2-3 minutes
5. Add broth, stir, making sure to scrape the bottom of the pan to remove any browned bits
6. Add tomatoes, cauliflower, pesto, salt and pepper
7. Lock lid and cook on HIGH pressure for 4 minutes
8. Release pressure naturally over 10 minutes
9. Use an immersion blender to puree the veggies in the soup
10. Turn Saute mode on and let the meat cook for a while, stir in cream and serve
11. Enjoy!

Nutrition Values (Per Serving)

- Calories: 441
- Fat: 30g
- Carbohydrates: 10g
- Protein: 30g

Elegant Fish Curry

(Prepping time: 5 minutes\ Cooking time: 4 minutes |For 4 servings)

Ingredients

- 2 tablespoons coconut oil
- 1 and ½ tablespoons fresh ginger, grated
- 2 teaspoons garlic, minced
- 1 tablespoon curry powder
- ½ teaspoon ground cumin
- 2 cups coconut milk
- 16 ounces firm white fish, cut into 1 inch chunks
- 1 cup kale, shredded
- 2 tablespoons cilantro, chopped

Directions

1. Pre-heat your Ninja Foodi to by selecting the Saute mode and setting the temperature to HIGH heat
2. Add coconut oil and let it heat up, add ginger and garlic and Saute for 2 minutes until light browned
3. Stir in curry powder, cumin, Saute for 2 minutes until fragrant
4. Stir in coconut milk, reduce heat to low and simmer for 5 minutes
5. Lock lid and cook on LOW pressure for 4 minutes
6. Release pressure naturally over 10 minutes
7. Stir in kale and cilantro, simmer in Saute mode for 2 minutes
8. Serve and enjoy!

Nutrition Values (Per Serving)

- Calories: 416
- Fat: 31g
- Carbohydrates: 5g
- Protein: 26g

Almond Cod Fillets

(Prepping time: 10 minutes\ Cooking time: 5-10 minutes |For 4 servings)

Ingredients

- 1 pound frozen cod fish fillets
- 2 garlic cloves, halved
- 1 cup chicken broth
- ½ cup packed parsley
- 2 tablespoons oregano

- 2 tablespoons almonds, sliced½ teaspoon paprika

Directions

1. Take the fish out of freezer and let it defrost
2. Take a food processor and stir in garlic, oregano, parsley, paprika, 1 tablespoon almond and process
3. Set your Ninja Foodi to "SAUTE" mode and add olive oil, let it heat up
4. Add remaining almonds and toast, transfer to a towel
5. Pour broth in pot and add herb mixture
6. Cut fish into 4 pieces and place in a steamer basket, transfer steamer basket to the pot
7. Lock lid and cook on HIGH pressure for 3 minutes
8. Quick release pressure once done
9. Serve steamer fish by pouring over the sauce
10. Enjoy!

Nutrition Values (Per Serving)

- Calories: 246
- Fat: 10g
- Carbohydrates: 8g
- Protein: 15g

Simple Sweet And Sour Fish Magnifico

(Prepping time: 10 minutes\ Cooking time: 6 minutes |For 4 servings)

Ingredients

- 2 drops liquid stevia
- ¼ cup butter
- 1 pound fish chunks
- 1 tablespoon vinegar
- Salt and pepper to taste

Directions

1. Set your Ninja Foodi to Saute mode and add butter, let it melt
2. Add fish chunks and Saute for 3 minutes
3. Add stevia, salt and pepper, stir
4. Lock Crisping Lid and cook on "Air Crisp" mode for 3 minutes at 360 degrees F
5. Serve once done and enjoy!

Nutrition Values (Per Serving)

- Calories: 274
- Fat: 15g

- Carbohydrates: 2g
- Protein: 33g

Cod With Broccoli, Lemon And Dill Mismash

(Prepping time: 15 minutes\ Cooking time: 2-5 minutes |For 4 servings)

Ingredients

- 1 pound, 1 inch thick frozen cod fillets
- 2 cups broccoli
- 1 cup water
- Dill weed
- Lemon pepper to taste
- Dash of salt

Directions

1. Cut fish into four pieces
2. Season fish pieces with lemon pepper, salt, dill weed
3. Add 1 cup water to the Ninja Foodi
4. Lower down steamer basket and add fish, broccoli florets to the steamer basket
5. Lock lid and cook on LOW pressure for 2 minutes
6. Quick release pressure
7. Serve and enjoy!

Nutrition Values (Per Serving)
- Calories: 463
- Fat: 33g
- Carbohydrates: 12g
- Protein: 25g

Butter Dredged "Rich" Lobster

(Prepping time: 15 minutes\ Cooking time: 20 minutes |For 4 servings)

Ingredients

- 6 Lobster Tails
- 4 garlic cloves,
- ¼ cup butter

Directions

13. Preheat the Ninja Foodi to 400 degrees F at first

14. Open the lobster tails gently by using kitchen scissors
15. Remove the lobster meat gently from the shells but keep it inside the shells
16. Take a plate and place it
17. Add some butter in a pan and allow it melt
18. Put some garlic cloves in it and heat it over medium-low heat
19. Pour the garlic butter mixture all over the lobster tail meat
20. Let the fryer to broil the lobster at 130 degrees F
21. Remove the lobster meat from Ninja Foodi and set aside
22. Use a fork to pull out the lobster meat from the shells entirely
23. Pour some garlic butter over it if needed
24. Serve and enjoy!

Nutrition Values (Per Serving)

- Calories: 160
- Fat: 1g
- Carbohydrates: 1g
- Protein: 20g

The Extremely Wild Alaskan Cod
(Prepping time: 10 minutes\ Cooking time: 5-10 minutes |For 4 servings)

Ingredients

- 1 large fillet, Alaskan Cod (Frozen)
- 1 cup cherry tomatoes
- Salt and pepper to taste
- Seasoning as you need
- 2 tablespoons butter
- Olive oil as needed

Directions

1. Take an ovenproof dish small enough to fit inside your pot
2. Add tomatoes to the dish, cut large fish fillet into 2-3 serving pieces and lay them on top of tomatoes
3. Season with salt, pepper and your seasoning
4. Top each fillet with 1 tablespoon butter and drizzle olive oil
5. Add 1 cup of water to the pot
6. Place trivet to the Ninja Foodi and place dish on the trivet
7. Lock lid and cook on HIGH pressure for 9 minutes
8. Release pressure naturally over 10 minutes
9. Serve and enjoy!

Nutrition Values (Per Serving)

- Calories: 449
- Fat: 32g
- Carbohydrates: 11g
- Protein: 25g

Magical Shrimp Platter

(Prepping time: 10 minutes\ Cooking time: 15 minutes |For 4 servings)

Ingredients

- 2 tablespoons butter
- ½ teaspoon smoked paprika
- 1 pound shrimp, peeled and deveined
- Lemongrass stalks
- 1 red chili pepper, seeded and chopped

Directions

1. Take a bowl and mix in all ingredients except lemongrass, let the mixture marinate for 60 minutes
2. Transfer the marinated fillet to your Ninja Foodi pot
3. Close lid and set to "Bake/Roast" mode and bake for 15 minutes at 345 degrees F
4. Serve and enjoy with a sprinkle of chopped lemon grass stalks
5. Enjoy!

Nutrition Values (Per Serving)

- Calories: 251
- Fat: 10g
- Carbohydrates: 3g
- Protein: 34g

Gentle Salmon Stew

(Prepping time: 5 minutes\ Cooking time: 11 minutes |For 4 servings)

Ingredients

- 1 cup fish broth
- Salt and pepper to taste
- 1 medium onion, chopped
- 1-2 pounds salmon fillets, cubed
- 1 tablespoon butter

Directions

1. Add the listed ingredients to a large sized bowl and let the shrimp marinate for 30-60 minutes
2. Grease the inner pot of the Ninja Foodi with butter and transfer marinated shrimp to the pot
3. Lock the lid and select "Bake/Roast" mode and bake for 15 minutes at 355 degrees F
4. Once done, serve and enjoy!

Nutrition Values (Per Serving)

- Calories: 173
- Fat: 8g
- Carbohydrates: 0.1g
- Protein: 23g

Chapter 8: Tasty Dessert Recipes

The Divine Fudge Delight

(Prepping time: 20 minutes\ Cooking time: 10 minutes
\ Freeze Time: 3-5 hours |For 24 servings)

Ingredients

- ½ teaspoon organic vanilla extract
- 1 cup heavy whipping cream
- 2 ounces butter, soft
- 2 ounces 70% dark chocolate, finely chopped

Directions

1. Set your Ninja-Foodi to Saute mode with "Medium-HIGH" temperature, add vanilla and heavy cream
2. Saute for 5 minutes and select "LOW" temperature
3. Saute for 10 minutes more, add butter and chocolate
4. Saute for 2 minutes more
5. Transfer the mix to a serving dish and refrigerate for a few hours
6. Serve chilled and enjoy!

Nutrition Values (Per Serving)

- Calories: 292
- Fat: 26g
- Carbohydrates: 8g
- Protein: 5g

Keto-Friendly Nut Porridge

(Prepping time: 10 minutes \ Cooking time: 10 minutes |For 4 servings)

Ingredients

- 4 teaspoons coconut oil, melted
- 1 cup pecans, halved
- 2 cups water
- 2 tablespoon stevia
- 1 cup cashew nuts, raw and unsalted

Directions

1. Add cashew nuts and pecans to your food processor and pulse until chunked

2. Add nuts mixture into pot and stir in water, coconut oil and stevia
3. Set your Ninja Foodi to sauté ode and add the nut mixture
4. Cook for 15 minutes
5. Serve immediately and enjoy!

Nutrition Values (Per Serving)

- Calories: 260
- Fat: 22g
- Carbohydrates: 8g
- Protein: 5g

Heartfelt Vanilla Yogurt

(Prepping time: 20 minutes and 9 hours culture time\ Cooking time: 3 hours |For 4 servings)

Ingredients

- ½ cup full-fat milk
- ¼ cup yogurt started
- 1 cup heavy cream
- ½ tablespoon pure vanilla extract
- 2 teaspoons stevia

Directions

1. Pour milk in your Ninja Foodi pot, stir in heavy cream, vanilla extract and Stevia
2. Let the yogurt sit and lock lid
3. Cook for 3 hours on "Slow Cooker" mode
4. Take a small bowl and mix 1 cup milk with yogurt starter, add this mixture to the pot
5. Lock lid and wrap the Foodi in two small t towels
6. Let it sit for 9 hours, allowing the yogurt to culture
7. Refrigerate and serve
8. Enjoy!

Nutrition Values (Per Serving)

- Calories: 292
- Fat: 26g
- Carbohydrates: 8g
- Protein: 5g

Delicious Lemon Mousse

(Prepping time: 10 minutes\ Cooking time: 12 minutes|For 2 servings)

Ingredients

- 1-2 ounces cream cheese, soft
- ½ cup heavy cream
- 1/8 cup fresh lemon juice
- ½ teaspoon lemon liquid stevia
- 2 pinch salt

Directions

1. Take a bowl and mix in cream cheese, heavy cream, lemon juice, salt and stevia
2. Pour the mixture into ramekins and transfer the ramekins to your Ninja Foodi pot
3. Lock lid and select "Bake/Roast" mode and bake for 12 minutes at 350 degrees F
4. Pour the mixture into

Nutrition Values (Per Serving)

- Calories: 292
- Fat: 26g
- Carbohydrates: 8g
- Protein: 5g

The Generous Strawberry Shortcake

(Prepping time: 10 minutes \ Cooking time: 15 minutes |For 4 servings)

Ingredients

- 1 whole egg
- ½ cup almond flour
- ½ teaspoon vanilla extract
- 1 tablespoon stevia
- 1 tablespoon ghee
- 3 tablespoons strawberries, chopped
- 1 cup water
- 3 tablespoons coconut whip cream

Directions

1. Add all ingredients except whip cream to a heat resistant mug, add a cup of water to the Ninja Foodi pot
2. Place steaming rack in your pot and place the mug in the rack

3. Lock lid and cook on HIGH pressure for 12 minutes
4. Quick release pressure
5. Remove lid and remove the mug
6. Top with coconut whipped cream and more strawberries
7. Enjoy!

Nutrition Values (Per Serving)

- Calories: 275
- Fat: 18g
- Carbohydrates: 3g
- Protein: 5g

Sensational Lemon Custard
(Prepping time: 10 minutes \ Cooking time: 22 minutes |For 4 servings)

Ingredients

- 5 egg yolks
- ¼ cup fresh squeeze lemon juice
- 1 tablespoon lemon zest
- 1 teaspoon pure vanilla extract
- 1/3 teaspoon liquid stevia
- 2 cups heavy cream
- 1 cup whipped coconut cream

Directions

1. Take a medium bowl and whisk in yolks, lemon juice, zest, vanilla and liquid stevia
2. Whisk in heavy cream and divide the mix between 4 (4 ounce sized) ramekins
3. Place the provided rack at the bottom of your Ninja Foodi
4. Place ramekins in rack
5. Add water just enough to reach halfway up the sides of ramekins
6. Lock lid and cook on HIGH pressure for 20 minutes
7. Quick release pressure
8. Remove ramekin and let it cool down to room temperature
9. Chill in fridge and serve topped up with whipped coconut cream
10. Enjoy!

Nutrition Values (Per Serving)

- Calories: 319
- Fat: 30g
- Carbohydrates: 3g

- Protein: 7g

Hearty Carrot Pumpkin Pudding

(Prepping time: 10 minutes\ Cooking time: 15 minutes |For 4 servings)

Ingredients

- 1 tablespoon extra-virgin olive oil
- 2 cups carrots, shredded
- 2 cups pureed pumpkin
- ½ sweet onion, finely chopped
- 1 cup heavy whip cream
- ½ cup cream cheese, soft
- 2 whole eggs
- 1 tablespoon granulated Erythritol
- 1 teaspoon ground nutmeg
- ½ teaspoon salt
- ¼ cup pumpkin seeds, garnish
- ¼ cup water

Directions

1. Add oil to your Ninja Foodi pot and whisk In carrots, pumpkin, onion, heavy cream, cream cheese, eggs, Erythritol, nutmeg, salt and water
2. Stir and lock lid
3. Cook on HIGH pressure for 10 minutes
4. Release pressure naturally over 10 minutes
5. Serve with a topping of pumpkin seeds
6. Enjoy!

Nutrition Values (Per Serving)

- Calories: 239
- Fat: 19g
- Carbohydrates: 7g
- Protein: 6g

Creative Crème Brulee

(Prepping time: 10 minutes + 3 hours chill time \ Cooking time: 15 minutes |For 4 servings)

Ingredients

- 1 cup heavy cream
- ½ tablespoons vanilla extract
- 3 egg yolks
- 1 pinch salt
- ¼ cup stevia

Directions

1. Take a bowl and mix in egg yolks, vanilla extract, salt and heavy cream
2. Mix well and beat until combined well
3. Divide the mixture between 4 greased ramekins evenly and transfer the ramekins to your Ninja Foodi
4. Lock lid and choose the "Bake/Roast" mode, bake for 35 minutes at 365 degrees F
5. Remove the ramekin from Ninja Foodi and wrap ramekins with plastic wrap
6. Refrigerate them to chill for about 3 hours
7. Serve and enjoy!

Nutrition Values (Per Serving)

- Calories: 260
- Fat: 22g
- Carbohydrates: 8g
- Protein: 5g

The Original Pot-De-Crème

(Prepping time: 15 minutes \ Cooking time: 15 minutes |For 4 servings)

Ingredients

- 6 egg yolks
- 2 cups heavy whip cream
- 1/3 cup cocoa powder
- 1 tablespoon pure vanilla extract
- ½ teaspoon liquid stevia
- Whipped coconut cream as needed for garnish
- Shaved dark chocolate, for garnish

Directions

1. Take a medium bowl and whisk in yolks, heavy cream, cocoa powder, vanilla and stevia
2. Pour the mixture into 1 and ½ quart baking dish and place the dish in your Ninja Foodi insert
3. Add enough water to reach about halfway up the sides of baking dish
4. Lock lid and cook on HIGH pressure for 12 minutes
5. Quick release pressure once the cycle is complete

6. Remove baking dish from insert and let it cool

7. Chill the dessert in refrigerator and serve with garnish of whipped coconut cream and shaved dark chocolate

8. Enjoy!

<u>Nutrition Values (Per Serving)</u>

- Calories: 275
- Fat: 18g
- Carbohydrates: 3g
- Protein: 5g

Chapter 9: Nice Snacks Recipes

Ultimate Creamy Zucchini Fries
(Prepping time: 10 minutes\ Cooking time: 10 minutes |For 4 servings)

Ingredients

- 1-2 pounds of zucchini, sliced into 2 and ½ inch sticks
- Salt to taste
- 1 cup cream cheese
- 2 tablespoons olive oil

Directions

1. Add zucchini in a colander and season with salt, add cream cheese and mix
2. Add oil into your Ninja Foodi's pot and add Zucchini
3. Lock Air Crisping Lid and set the temperature to 365 degrees F and timer to 10 minutes
4. Let it cook for 10 minutes and take the dish out once done, enjoy!

Nutrition Values (Per Serving)

- Calories: 374
- Fat: 36g
- Carbohydrates: 6g
- Protein: 7g

Inspiring Cauliflower Hash Browns
(Prepping time: 10 minutes\ Cooking time: 30 minutes |For 6 servings)

Ingredients

- 6 whole eggs
- 4 cups cauliflower rice
- ¼ cup milk
- 1 onion, chopped
- 3 tablespoons butter
- 1 and ½ cups cooked ham, chopped
- ½ cup shredded cheese

Directions

1. Set your Ninja Foodi to sauté mode and add butter, let the butter heat up
2. Add onions and cook for 5 minutes until tender. Add iced cauliflower to pot and stir

3. Lock the Air Crisping lid and Air Crisp for 15 minutes, making sure to give them a turn about halfway through

4. Take a small bowl and mix in eggs and milk, pour mixture over browned cauliflower

5. Sprinkle ham over top. Press Air Crispy again and crisp for 10 minutes more

6. Sprinkle cheddar cheese on top and lock lid, let the crisp for 1 minute more until the cheese melts. Serve and enjoy!

Nutrition Values (Per Serving)

- Calories: 166
- Fat: 14g
- Carbohydrates: 3g
- Protein: 9g

Everybody's Favorite Cauliflower Patties

(Prepping time: 5 minutes \ Cooking time: 20 minutes |For 4 servings)

Ingredients

- 3 whole eggs
- 1 chili pepper, chopped
- ½ teaspoon garlic powder
- Salt and pepper to taste
- 2 cups cauliflower, chopped
- ¾ cups olive oil
- ¼ cup cheddar cheese
- ¼ cup whole mozzarella cheese

Directions

1. Cut cauliflower into small florets, remove leaves and cut out a core

2. Add 1 cup water to Ninja Food, transfer florets to steamer basket and place it on a trivet in your Ninja Foodi. Lock lid and cook on HIGH pressure for 5 minutes

3. Mash steamed cauliflower and dry them, add shredded cheese, eggs, chili, salt and pepper

4. Mix well and shape into flat patties

5. Heat up oil in your Ninja Foodi and set to Saute mode, shallow fry patties until crisp on both sides. Serve and enjoy!

Nutrition Values (Per Serving)

- Calories: 550
- Fat: 54g
- Carbohydrates: 5g
- Protein: 13g

Kale And Almonds Mix

(Prepping time: 10 minutes \ Cooking time: 4 minutes |For 4 servings)

Ingredients

- 1 cup of water
- 1 big kale bunch, chopped
- 1 tablespoon balsamic vinegar
- 1/3 cup toasted almonds
- 3 garlic cloves, minced
- 1 small yellow onion, chopped
- 2 tablespoons olive oil

Directions

1. Set your Ninja Foodi on Saute mode and add oil, let it heat up
2. Stir in onion and cook for 3 minutes. Add garlic, water, kale, and stir
3. Lock lid and cook on HIGH pressure for 4 minutes. Quick release pressure
4. Add salt, pepper, vinegar, almonds and toss well. Serve and enjoy!

Nutrition Values (Per Serving)

- Calories: 140
- Fat: 6g
- Carbohydrates: 5g
- Protein: 3g

Simple Treat Of Garlic

(Prepping time: 10 minutes \ Cooking time: 5 minutes |For 4 servings)

Ingredients

- 1 tablespoon extra-virgin olive oil
- 2 garlic cloves, minced
- 2 large-sized Belgian endive, halved lengthwise
- ½ cup apple cider vinegar
- ½ cup broth
- Salt and pepper to taste
- 1 teaspoon cayenne pepper

Directions

1. Set your Ninja Foodi to Saute mode and add oil, let the oil heat up

2. Add garlic and cook for 30 seconds unto browned

3. Add endive, vinegar, broth, salt, pepper, and cayenne

4. Lock lid and cook on LOW pressure for 2 minutes. Quick release pressure and serve. Enjoy!

Nutrition Values (Per Serving)

- Calories: 91
- Fat: 6g
- Carbohydrates: 3g
- Protein: 2g

Buttered Up Garlic And Fennel

(Prepping time: 10 minutes \ Cooking time: 5 minutes |For 4 servings)

Ingredients

- ½ stick butter
- 2 garlic cloves, sliced
- ½ teaspoon salt
- 1 and ½ pounds fennel bulbs, cut into wedges
- ¼ teaspoon ground black pepper
- ½ teaspoon cayenne
- ¼ teaspoon dried dill weed
- 1/3 cup dry white wine
- 2/3 cup stock

Directions

1. Set your Ninja Foodi to Saute mode and add butter, let it heat up

2. Add garlic and cook for 30 seconds. Add rest of the ingredients

3. Lock lid and cook on LOW pressure for 3 minutes. Remove lid and serve. Enjoy!

Nutrition Values (Per Serving)

- Calories: 111
- Fat: 6g
- Carbohydrates: 2g
- Protein: 2g

Obvious Paprika And Cabbage

(Prepping time: 10 minutes \ Cooking time: 4 minutes |For 4 servings)

Ingredients

- 1 and ½ pounds green cabbage, shredded
- Salt and pepper to taste
- 3 tablespoon ghee
- 1 cup vegetable stock
- ¼ teaspoon sweet paprika

Directions

1. Set your Ninja Foodi to Saute mode and add ghee, let it melt
2. Add cabbage, salt, pepper, and stock, stir well
3. Lock lid and cook on HIGH pressure for 7 minutes. Quick release pressure
4. Add paprika and toss well. Divide between plates and serve. Enjoy!

Nutrition Values (Per Serving)

- Calories: 170
- Fat: 4g
- Carbohydrates: 5g
- Protein: 5g

Authentic Western Omelet

(Prepping time: 5 minutes\ Cooking time: 34 minutes |For 2 servings)

Ingredients

- 3 eggs, whisked
- 3 ounces chorizo, chopped
- 1-ounces Feta cheese, crumbled
- 5 tablespoons almond milk
- ¾ teaspoon chili flakes
- ¼ teaspoon salt
- 1 green pepper, chopped

Directions

1. Add all the ingredients and mix them well. Stir it gently. Take an omelet pan and pour the mixture into it. Preheat your Ninja Foodi at "Roast/Bake" mode at 320 F.
2. Cook for 4 minutes. After that, transfer the pan with an omelet in Ninja Foodi
3. Cook for 30 minutes more at the same mode. Serve hot and enjoy!

Nutrition Values (Per Serving)

- Calories: 426
- Fat: 38.2g

- Carbohydrates: 6.8g
- Protein: 21.7g

Bowl Full Of Broccoli Salad

(Prepping time: 10 minutes \ Cooking time: 5 minutes |For 4 servings)

Ingredients

- 1 pound broccoli, cut into florets
- 2 tablespoons balsamic vinegar
- 2 garlic cloves, minced
- 1 teaspoon mustard seeds
- 1 teaspoon cumin seeds
- Salt and pepper to taste
- 1 cup cottage cheese, crumbled

Directions

1. Add 1 cup water to your Ninja Foodi. Place steamer basket
2. Place broccoli in basket and lock lid, cook on HIGH pressure for 5 minutes
3. Quick release pressure and remove lid. Toss broccoli with other ingredients and serve. Enjoy!

Nutrition Values (Per Serving)

- Calories: 95
- Fat: 3.1g
- Carbohydrates: 10g
- Protein: 2g

Rise And Shine Breakfast Casserole

(Prepping time: 10 minutes\ Cooking time: 10 minutes |For 6 servings)

Ingredients

- 4 whole eggs
- 1 tablespoons milk
- 1 cup ham, cooked and chopped
- ½ cup cheddar cheese, shredded

- ¼ teaspoon salt
- ¼ teaspoon ground black pepper

Directions

1. Take a baking pan (small enough to fit into your Ninja Foodi) bowl, and grease it well with butter. Take a medium bowl and whisk in eggs, milk, salt, pepper and add ham, cheese, and stir. Pour mixture into baking pan and lower the pan into your Ninja Foodi
2. Set your Ninja Foodi Air Crisp mode and Air Crisp for 325 degrees F for 7 minutes
3. Remove pan from eggs and enjoy!

Nutrition Values (Per Serving)

- Calories: 169
- Fat: 13g
- Carbohydrates: 1g
- Protein: 12g

Cauliflower And Egg Dish

(Prepping time: 10 minutes \ Cooking time: 4 minutes |For 4 servings)

Ingredients

- 21 ounces cauliflower, separated into florets
- 1 cup red onion, chopped
- 1 cup celery, chopped
- ½ cup of water
- Salt and pepper to taste
- 2 tablespoons balsamic vinegar
- 1 teaspoon stevia
- 4 boiled eggs, chopped
- 1 cup Keto Friendly mayonnaise

Directions

1. Add water to Ninja Foodi
2. Add steamer basket and add cauliflower, lock lid and cook on High Pressure for 5 minutes
3. Quick release pressure. Transfer cauliflower to bowl and add eggs, celery, onion and toss
4. Take another bowl and mix in mayo, salt, pepper, vinegar, stevia and whisk well
5. Add a salad, toss well. Divide into salad bowls and serve. Enjoy!

Nutrition Values (Per Serving)

- Calories: 170
- Fat: 4g

- Carbohydrates: 5g
- Protein: 5g

Just A Simple Egg Frittata

(Prepping time: 10 minutes \ Cooking time: 15 minutes |For 4 servings)

Ingredients

- 5 whole eggs
- ¾ teaspoon mixed herbs
- 1 cup spinach
- ¼ cup shredded cheddar cheese
- ½ cup mushrooms
- Salt and pepper to taste
  ¾ cup half and half
  2 tablespoons butter

Directions

1. Dice mushrooms, chop spinach finely
2. Set your Ninja Foodi to Saute mode and add spinach, mushrooms
3. Whisk eggs, milk, cream cheese, herbs, and Sautéed vegetables in a bowl and mix well
4. Take a 6-inch baking pan and grease it well
5. Pour mixture and transfer to your Ninja Foodie (on a trivet)
6. Cook on HIGH pressure for 2 minutes. Quick release pressure. Serve and enjoy!

Nutrition Values (Per Serving)

- Calories: 300
- Fat: 25g
- Carbohydrates: 5g
- Protein: 14g

Ultimate Cheese Dredged Cauliflower Snack

(Prepping time: 10 minutes\ Cooking time: 30 minutes |For 4 servings)

Ingredients

- 1 tablespoon mustard
- 1 head cauliflower
- 1 teaspoon avocado mayonnaise
- ½ cup parmesan cheese, grated

- ¼ cup butter, cut into small pieces

Directions

1. Set your Ninja Foodi to Saute mode and add butter and cauliflower
2. Saute for 3 minutes. Add remaining ingredients and stir
3. Lock lid and cook on HIGH pressure for 30 minutes. Release pressure naturally over 10 minutes
4. Serve and enjoy!

Nutrition Values (Per Serving)

- Calories: 155
- Fat: 13g
- Carbohydrates: 4g
- Protein: 6g

The Onion And Smoky Mushroom Medley
(Prepping time: 5 minutes\ Cooking time: 2 minutes |For 4 servings)

Ingredients

- 1 tablespoon ghee
- 1 carton (8 ounces) button mushrooms, sliced
- 1 onion, diced
- ½ teaspoon salt
- 2 tablespoon coconut aminos
- 1/8 teaspoon smoked paprika

Directions

1. Set your Ninja Foodi to Saute mode and add ghee, let it heat up
2. Add mushrooms, onion and seasoning, Saute for 5 minutes
3. Lock lid and cook on HIGH pressure for 3 minutes
4. Quick release pressure
5. Serve warm and enjoy!

Nutrition Values (Per Serving)

- Calories: 268
- Fat: 20g
- Carbohydrates: 11g
- Protein: 10g

Cool Beet Chips
(Prepping time: 10 minutes\ Cooking time: 8 hours |For 8 servings)

Ingredients

- ½ beet, peeled and cut into 1/8 inch slices

Directions

1. Arrange beet slices in single layer in the Cook and Crisp basket
2. Place the basket in the pot and close the crisping lid
3. Press the Dehydrate button and let it dehydrate for 8 hours at 135 degrees F
4. Once the dehydrating is done, remove the basket from pot and transfer slices to your Air Tight container, serve and enjoy!

Nutrition Values (Per Serving)

- Calories: 35
- Fat: 0g
- Carbohydrates: 8g
- Protein: 1g

Lovely Cauliflower Soup

(Prepping time: 10 minutes\ Cooking time:301 minutes |For 5 servings)

Ingredients

- 5 slices bacon, chopped
- 1 onion, chopped
- 3 garlic cloves, minced
- 1 cauliflower head, trimmed
- 4 cups chicken broth
- 1 cup almond milk
- 1 teaspoon salt
- 1 teaspoon black pepper
- 1 and ½ cups cheddar cheese, shredded
- Sour cream and chopped fresh chives for serving

Directions

1. Set your pot to Saute mode and pre-heat it for 5 minutes on HIGH settings
2. Add bacon, onion, garlic to your pot and cook for 5 minutes
3. Reserve bacon for garnish
4. Add cauliflower, chicken broth to the pot and place pressure cooker lid, seal the pressure valves
5. Cook on HIGH pressure for 10 minutes, quick release the pressure once did
6. Add milk, and mash the soup reaches your desired consistency
7. Season with salt, pepper and sprinkle cheese evenly on top of the soup
8. Close crisping lid and Broil for 5 minutes

9. Once done, top with reserved crispy bacon and serve with sour cream and chives
10. Enjoy!

Nutrition Values (Per Serving)

- Calories: 253
- Fat: 17g
- Carbohydrates: 12g
- Protein: 13g

Elegant Broccoli Pops
(Prepping time: 60 minutes\ Cooking time: 12 minutes |For 4 servings)

Ingredients

- 1/3 cup parmesan cheese, grated
- 2 cups cheddar cheese, grated
- Salt and pepper to taste
- 3 eggs, beaten
- 3 cups broccoli florets
- 1 tablespoon olive oil

Directions

1. Add broccoli into a food processor and pulse until finely crumbed
2. Transfer broccoli to a large sized bowl and add remaining ingredients to the bowl, mix well
3. Make small balls using the mixture and let them chill for 30 minutes
4. Place balls in your Ninja Foodi pot and Air Crisping lid
5. Let it cook for 12 minutes at 365 degrees F on the "Air Crisp" mode
6. Once done, remove and enjoy!

Nutrition Values (Per Serving)

- Calories: 162
- Fat: 12g
- Carbohydrates: 2g
- Protein: 12g

Great Brussels Bite
(Prepping time: 5 minutes\ Cooking time: 3 minutes |For 4 servings)

Ingredients

- 1 pound Brussels sprouts
- ¼ cup pine nuts
- Salt and pepper to taste
- Olive oil as needed
- 1 cup water

Directions

1. Place a steamer basket in your Ninja Foodi and add Brussels to the basket
2. Add water and lock lid, cook on HIGH pressure for 3 minutes
3. Quick release pressure
4. Transfer Brussels to a plate and toss with olive oil, salt ,pepper and sprinkle of pine nuts
5. Enjoy!

Nutrition Values (Per Serving)

- Calories: 112
- Fat: 7g
- Carbohydrates: 4g
- Protein: 5g

Simple Mushroom Saute

(Prepping time: 10 minutes\ Cooking time: 15 minutes |For 8 servings)

Ingredients

- 1 pound white mushrooms, stems trimmed
- 2 tablespoons unsalted butter
- ½ teaspoon salt
- ¼ cup water

Directions

1. Quarter medium mushrooms and cut any large mushrooms into eight

2. Put mushrooms, butter, and salt in your Foodi's inner pot

3. Add water and lock pressure lid, making sure to seal the valve

4. Cook on HIGH pressure for 5 minutes, quick release pressure once did

5. Once done, set your pot to Saute mode on HIGH mode and bring the mix to a boil over 5 minutes until all the water evaporates

6. Once the butter/water has evaporated, stir for 1 minute until slightly browned

7. Enjoy!

Nutrition Values (Per Serving)

- Calories: 50
- Fat: 4g
- Carbohydrates: 2g
- Protein: 2g

Delicious Assorted Nuts

(Prepping time: 5 minutes\ Cooking time: 15 minutes |For 4 servings)

Ingredients

- 1 tablespoon butter, melted
- ½ cup raw cashew nuts
- 1 cup raw almonds
- Salt to taste

Directions

1. Add nuts to your Ninja Foodi pot
2. Lock lid and cook on "Air Crisp" mode for 10 minutes at 350 degrees F
3. Remove nuts into a bowl and add melted butter and salt
4. Toss well to coat
5. Return the mix to your Ninja Foodi, lock lid and bake for 5 minutes on BAKE/ROAST mode
6. Serve and enjoy!

Nutrition Values (Per Serving)

- Calories: 189
- Fat: 16g
- Carbohydrates: 7g
- Protein: 7g

Garlic And Sage Spaghetti Squash

(Prepping time: 5 minutes\ Cooking time: 17 minutes |For 4 servings)

Ingredients

- 1 spaghetti squash, halved crosswise and seeded
- 2 teaspoons stevia
- ¼ teaspoon salt
- 1/8 teaspoon black pepper
- 1/8 teaspoon crushed red pepper flakes
- 1/5 cup unsalted butter
- 2 cloves garlic, thinly sliced
- 12 fresh sage leaves

Directions

1. Place steamer insert in your Ninja Foodi
2. Add 1 and ½ cup water to the pot
3. Place spaghetti squash halves on steamer rack and lock lid, cook on HIGH pressure for 12 minutes
4. Quick release pressure
5. Take a small bowl and add stevia, salt, pepper , pepper flakes and mix
6. Life squash out and shred using 2 forks, pour water out of pot and dry it
7. Set your pot to Saute mode and add butter, let it heat up
8. Add garlic, cook for 1 and ½ minutes
9. Add sage and stevia mixture, cook for 45 seconds
10. Pour the prepared sauce over spaghetti and stir
11. Enjoy!

Nutrition Values (Per Serving)

- Calories: 214
- Fat: 20g
- Carbohydrates: 5g
- Protein: 5g

Spicy Cauliflower Steak

(Prepping time: 5 minutes\ Cooking time: 5 minutes |For 4 servings)

Ingredients

- 1 large cauliflower head
- 2 tablespoons extra virgin olive oil
- 2 teaspoons paprika
- 2 teaspoons ground cumin
- ¾ teaspoon kosher salt
- ¼ cup fresh cilantro, chopped
- 1 lemon quartered

Directions

1. Place a steamer insert in your pot and add 1 and ½ cups water to the pot
2. Remove leaves form cauliflower and trim the core so the leaves sit flat
3. Transfer to rack
4. Take a small bowl and add olive oil, paprika, cumin and salt
5. Drizzle the mix over cauliflower and rub
6. Lock lid and cook on HIGH pressure for 4 minutes, quick release pressure
7. Once done, open up the lid and transfer the cooked cauliflower to a cutting board
8. Slice into 1 inch thick steaks and divide them amongst serving plates
9. Sprinkle cilantro, serve with lemon quarters and enjoy!

Nutrition Values (Per Serving)

- Calories: 268
- Fat: 23g
- Carbohydrates: 10g
- Protein: 5g

Subtle Buffalo Chicken Meatballs

(Prepping time: 10 minutes\ Cooking time: 40 minutes |For 6 servings)

Ingredients

- 1 pound chicken, ground
- 1 carrot, minced
- 2 celery stalks, minced
- ¼ cup blue cheese, crumbled
- ¼ cup buffalo sauce (check for Keto friendliness)
- 1 whole egg
- ¼ cup almond meal
- 2 tablespoons extra virgin olive oil
- ½ cup water

Directions

1. Set your Ninja to Saute mode and set it to HIGH, let it pre-heated for 5 minutes
2. Take a large mixing bowl and add chicken, carrot, celery, blue cheese, buffalo sauce, almond meal, egg. Mix and shape the mixture into 1 and ½ inch balls
3. Pour olive oil into your pot, and add the meatballs in batches, sear until all sides are browned. Keep the seared balls on the side
4. Place Cook and Crisp Basket in the pot and add water, add the seared meatballs
5. Place pressure lid and seal the pressure valves
6. Cook on HIGH pressure for 5 minutes, quick release the pressure once did
7. Close crisping lid and cook for 10 minutes at 360 degrees F
8. After 5 minutes of cooking, open the lid and lift the basket to give it a shake, lower it back and continue cooking
9. Enjoy once done!

Nutrition Values (Per Serving)

- Calories: 204
- Fat: 13g
- Carbohydrates: 5g
- Protein: 16g

The Original Steamed Artichoke

(Prepping time: 5 minutes\ Cooking time: 25 minutes |For 4 servings)

Ingredients

- 2 medium sized whole artichokes
- 1 lemon wedge
- 1 cup water

Directions

1. Rinse artichokes under water and clean it, remove any damaged outer leaves
2. Take a sharp knife and trim off stem and top third of each choke
3. Rub the cut with lemon wedge to prevent browning
4. Add 1 cup water to your Foodi and place steamer basket in the pot, add artichokes to the rack
5. Lock lid and cook on HIGH pressure for 20 minutes
6. Release pressure naturally over 10 minutes
7. Open lid and transfer to plate
8. Serve and enjoy!

Nutrition Values (Per Serving)

- Calories: 564
- Fat: 40g
- Carbohydrates: 5g
- Protein: 2g

Crispy Avocado Chips

(Prepping time: 10 minutes\ Cooking time: 10 minutes |For 4 servings)

Ingredients

- 4 tablespoons butter
- 4 raw avocados, peeled and sliced into chips form
- Salt and pepper to taste

Directions

1. Season avocado slices with salt and pepper
2. Grease the pot of your Ninja Foodi with butter and add the avocado slices
3. Lock Crisping lid and cook on "Air Crisp" mode for 10 minutes at 350 degrees F
4. Remove the dish from Ninja Foodi and serve, enjoy!

Nutrition Values (Per Serving)

- Calories: 391
- Fat: 38g
- Carbohydrates: 15g
- Protein: 3.5g

The Crazy Egg-Stuffed Avocado Dish

(Prepping time: 10 minutes\ Cooking time: 5 minutes |For 6 servings)

Ingredients

- ½ tablespoon fresh lemon juice
- 1 medium ripe avocado, peeled, pitted and chopped
- 6 organic eggs, boiled, peeled and cut in half lengthwise
- Salt to taste
- ½ cup fresh watercress, trimmed

Directions

1. Place steamer basket at the bottom of your Ninja Foodie
2. Add water
3. Add watercress on the basket and lock lid
4. Cook on HIGH pressure for 3 minutes, quick release the pressure and drain the watercress
5. Remove egg yolks and transfer them to a bowl
6. Add watercress, avocado, lemon juice, salt into the bowl and mash with fork
7. Place egg whites in a serving bowl and fill them with the watercress and avocado dish
8. Serve and enjoy!

Nutrition Values (Per Serving)

- Calories: 132
- Fat: 10g
- Carbohydrates: 3g
- Protein: 5g

Conclusion

I can't express how honored I am to think that you found my book interesting and informative enough to read it all through to the end.

I thank you again for purchasing this book and I hope that you had as much fun reading it as I had writing it.

I bid you farewell and encourage you to move forward with your amazing Ninja Foodi!

Appendix 1: Measurement Conversion Table

Volume Equivalents (Liquid)

US Standard	US Standard (Ounces)	Metric (Approximate)
2 tablespoons	1 fl. oz.	30 mL
¼ cup	2 fl. oz.	60mL
½ cup	4 fl. oz.	120mL
1 cup	8 fl. oz.	240 mL
1 and ½ cups	12 fl. oz.	355 mL
2 cups/1 pint	16 fl. oz.	475 mL
4 cups/ 1 quart	32 fl. oz.	1 L
1 gallon	128 fl. oz.	4L

Volume Equivalents (Dry)

US Standard	Metric (Approximate)
1/8 teaspoon	0.5 mL
¼ teaspoon	1 mL
½ teaspoon	2 mL
¾ teaspoon	4 mL
1 teaspoon	5 mL
1 tablespoon	15 mL
¼ cup	59 mL
1/3 cup	79 mL
½ cup	118 mL
2/3 cup	156 mL
¾ cup	177 mL
1 cup	235 mL
2 cups	475 mL
3 cups	700 mL
4 cups	1 L

Oven Temperatures

Fahrenheit (F)	Celsius (C) (Approximate)
250°	120°
300°	150°
325°	165°
350°	180°
375°	190°

400°	200°
425°	220°
450°	230°

Weight Equivalents

US Standard	Metric (Approximate)
½ ounce	15 g
1 ounce	30 g
2 ounces	60 g
4 ounces	115 g
8 ounces	225 g
12 ounces	340 g
16 ounces/1 pound	455 g

Appendix II: Healthy Food List For Weight Loss And Keto

Nowadays, too many people want to lose weight and get healthy! Keto Diet has many followers in this world. If you are one of the followers, while you are on a Keto Diet, you should consider keeping the following ingredients in your plate in order to get maximum benefits from your diet!

- Seafood such as Salmon, Mussels, Clams, Oysters, Mackerel, Sardines etc.
- Low carb veggies such as Brussels, spinach, broccoli, cauliflower, zucchini etc.
- Various types of healthy cheese that are rich in calcium, protein and essential fatty acids
- Avocados
- Fresh meat and chicken/poultry. Try to opt for Grass-Fed meat as much as possible
- Eggs
- Coconut Oil
- Cottage Cheese/ Plain Greek Yogurt
- Olive Oil
- Various types of nuts and seeds such as Brazil Nuts, Almonds, Cashews, Pecans, Macadamia, Pistachio, Walnuts, Chia Seeds, Flaxseeds etc.
- Various kinds of berries such as Strawberries, Blueberries, Blackberries, Raspberries
- Cream and Butter
- Shirataki Noodles
- Olives
- Unsweetened Tea and Coffee (in controlled amounts)
- Dark Chocolate and Cocoa Powder

Those are the ingredients that you should try to keep around as much as possible. Asides from that, below is a full list of the all food that allowed or restricted while on a Keto Diet.

Meats And Animal Produce: While choosing your meat, always make sure to avoid farmed animal meats and processed meats such as sausages or hot dogs.

Try to go for the animal meats and animal-derived products:

- Offal from grass-fed animals: kidney, liver, tripe, tongue, etc
- Butter
- Gelatin
- Ghee
- Pastured eggs
- Pastured poultry and pork
- Seafood caught in the wild such as caviar, crab, mussels, clams, and scallops
- Wild caught fish such as cod, mackerel, tuna, eel, etc.
- Grass-fed meat such as lamb, venison, beef, lamb, chicken, rabbit, etc.

Fats: Try to take more saturated and Monosaturated varieties of fat.

- Saturated fats include lard, tallow, duck fat, chicken fat, ghee, etc.
- Monounsaturated fats include avocado oil, olive oil, and macadamia oil

- Fats rich in poly-saturated Omega-3s extracted from animal sources
- Cocoa butter, coconut butter
- 90% or higher dark chocolate
- Palm shortening
- Chia seeds

Vegetables: When choosing your vegetable, try to avoid root vegetables and stick to the green leafy ones as they will help you to keep your carbohydrates level at a minimum.

- Watercress
- Zucchini
- Spinach
- Tomatoes
- Shallots
- Seaweeds
- Pumpkin
- Scallions
- Radishes
- Okra
- Onions
- Mushrooms
- All leafy greens
- Lettuce
- Garlic
- Fennel
- Cucumber
- Chives
- Cauliflower
- Chives
- Celery
- Carrots
- Cabbage
- Broccoli
- Bell Pepper
- Asparagus
- Artichokes

Fruits: Regarding a Ketogenic diet, most fruits are off the table, mainly because of the high level of fructose. However, small amounts of berries are allowed.
Good choices for fruits are:

- Avocado
- Olives

- Blackberry
- Lime
- Lemon
- Blueberry
- Raspberry
- Strawberry
- Cranberry

Legumes: Similar to fruits, all types of legumes are off the table. However, a very small amount of peas or green beans can be included in your diet.

Dairy Products: In general, the following dairy products are good for your soul

- Kefir
- Full fat yogurt
- Full fat raw cheese
- Full fat cottage cheese
- Heavy whipping cream
- Full fat sour cream
- Full fat cream cheese
- Ghee
- Butter

Drinks: All types of sweet or aerated drinks are to be avoided entirely in your Keto diet. Drink of plenty of water though! Good drinks include:

- Coconut milk
- Almond milk
- Cashew milk
- Broth and soups
- Herbal teas
- Coffee teas
- Water
- Seltzer water
- Club soda
- Lemon and lime juices
- Sparkline water
- Water

Nuts and Seeds: In general nuts and seeds are allowed, but you should try to keep your intake at low levels since they enhance your carbohydrate intake. Be cautious while consuming nuts. However, keep In mind that you are to avoid peanuts as they fall under the legume category.
The following are allowed though:

- Almonds

- Macadamias
- Hazelnuts
- Pecans
- Pistachios
- Pine nuts
- Pumpkin seeds
- Sesame seeds
- Psyllium seeds
- Sunflower seeds
- Cashew nuts
- Walnuts
- Chia seeds

Herbs And Spices: As for herbs and spices, you are allowed to experiment with a wide variety of spices and herbs to enhance the flavor of your meals. Just make sure to avoid store-bought spices and herb that have hidden sugars of MSG's as they would break your Keto diet.

Recommended spices include:

- Black pepper
- White pepper
- Sea salt
- Basil
- Chili powder
- Curry powder
- Italian seasoning
- Cumin powder
- Oregano
- Thyme
- Sage
- Rosemary
- Turmeric
- Parsley
- Cilantro
- Cinnamon
- Cloves
- Allspices
- Paprika
- Ginger
- Cardamom

CPSIA information can be obtained
at www.ICGtesting.com
Printed in the USA
LVHW101144191021
700840LV00002BA/60